ReShaping Faith™

One Chaplain Visit at A Time

ReShaping Faith™

One Chaplain Visit at A Time

Chaplain Dorcus Cater, MDIV., BCC

ReShaping Faith™ is a trademark of Reshaping Faith Publishing, LLC

Cataloging-in-Publication data on file with the Library of Congress

ISBN: 979-8-9929991-0-5

ISBN: 979-8-9929991-1-2

eISBN: 979-8-9929991-2-9

Library of Congress Control Number: 2025907552

Published in the United States by

ReShaping Faith Publishing, LLC
4002 Highway 78, Suite 530-213
Snellville, Georgia 30039 USA
www.reshapingfaith.com

Cover design by Dorcus Cater

Dedication

To my father, Albert Crumbley AKA Dada, my first love and the chaplain who trained me by example to meet the needs of the poor in resources, as well as the poor in spirit. And to my husband, Darrell Cater, who has remained a force of emotional stability and steadfast support.

Author's Note

The chaplain encounters in this book are not in chronological order. Also, the details about the spiritual care seekers and their families are extremely altered to protect the anonymity of the family members possibly left behind. Lastly, I believe in the Holy Trinity, God in three persons: God the Father, God the Son (Jesus), and God the Holy Spirit. Different names (Father, Abba, Lord, Savior, Holy Spirit, Jesus, etc.) for all three will be used interchangeably throughout this book.

Table of Contents

Introduction 1

Section One: Plot Twist 4

    Chapter 1: Rescue Mission 5

    Chapter 2: Surprised by Death 15

    Chapter 3: Rerouted 21

    Chapter 4: Unpopular Pardons 29

Section Two: Inconvenient Truth 38

    Chapter 5: Little God 39

    Chapter 6: Misguided Alliance 47

    Chapter 7: Bite of Death 51

    Chapter 8: Opt-Out 55

Section Three: Interrupted by Love 62

    Chapter 9: The Sons and Daughters Of Abraham 63

    Chapter 10: The Doctor 69

    Chapter 11: The Engineer 73

    Chapter 12: The Congressman 77

Section Four: The Cost 86

    Chapter 13: Wicked Witnesses 87

    Chapter 14: Service Connection 95

    Chapter 15: Identity Crisis 99

    Chapter 16: Questionable Companionship 107

Section Five: Golden Girls..112

    Chapter 17: Scorned Woman 113

    Chapter 18: Grief Growl 119

    Chapter 19: Sound of Despair..125

    Chapter 20: Faulty Faith 129

    Chapter 21: Overcomer..139

    Author's Info..151

Introduction

A late bloomer, I discerned the call of God for me to enter professional ministry later in life. As a Christian Believer, I had always felt a pull, of sorts, but no clear understanding of what it meant. So, I was excited when I finally got an official invitation from the God of the Bible that I was willing to run with.

I didn't know what the "call" meant, but I felt that whatever it meant, among other things, I needed something more to answer, so I enrolled in seminary. I understood that I was narrow-minded, and I was okay with it, but if I was going to serve others, I needed to expand my perspectives. I thought seminary was my way to expansion, and it was. Professional chaplaincy was birthed in me, thereby kickstarting my path to a more unbiased and enlightened approach to spirituality.

Nevertheless, my time in seminary was very challenging. It stands out as one of the more difficult times of my adult life. When I began my seminary journey, I was sure that Jesus was the *only* way to God. I am not sure when it happened, but at some point, I began to consider that maybe He was not.

My questioning was likely due to the different faith traditions and brands of Christianity represented by the student body, as well as the faculty at the Baptist seminary. How can all these educated people be wrong, I considered. My educational journey was quite choppy. With God's help, I completed my master's level seminary career in three years, but I was in and out of college for twenty years before completing my bachelor's degree. I understood that there were likely gaps in my perspective and how I viewed the world, so I was receptive to embracing new ways of believing.

During my time in seminary, I began to question aspects of the Bible narrative, but I realized that it was not the beginning of my questioning of such. The questions weren't new, but in the past, I did not have the courage to acknowledge or to confront them. Seminary granted me permission to take a more critical look at my faith and the Bible narrative.

As a result, I basically stopped reading and using the Bible as my primary source of spiritual enrichment. The new voices in my head had too many adversarial things to say about it, so I turned them down by not reading the Bible as much. I never made a conscious decision to do such. It just happened. By the end of my three years in seminary, I still wasn't sure if Jesus was the *only* way, but I was still sure that He is the *only* way for me.

It wasn't possible for me to unknow the Jesus who had introduced Himself to me twenty-two years prior to seminary and had walked with me up to that point. I couldn't unknow the countless ways that Jesus had shown up for me. Regardless of what anyone else believed, Jesus was the *only* way for me, and that was enough for me. I graduated seminary and left it at that.

Two years later, I was on a spiritual fast when the Holy Spirit revealed that my new critical way of looking at the Holy Scriptures was more sinister than I knew. Of course, I was not aware of what had happened to me. I was ignorantly proud of my new critical spirit and my unwillingness to accept the claims of infallibility regarding the Bible. The new critical spirit was a token of my higher learning, but the Holy Spirit was unwilling to leave me there.

Jesus interrupted my state of unbelief and delivered me from the voices of unbelief and confusion that had attached themselves to me in seminary. I felt "belief" return to me, and I had an instant knowing that I was being delivered. I understood in that moment that the God of the Bible, the only true God is and has always been honorable in every way in His dealings with humankind, Scripturally and in every other way, whether I understood it fully or not. I was comforted by the reality that we don't always have a full understanding of a thing all at once, and it's by the Father's design. It is the mercy of God that our journey to Jesus, the Truth is primarily incremental and customized for each one of us individually.

Simply put, our God is out of this world. The human mind cannot fully contain God's precepts or wisdom without exploding. Who can know the mind of God? I was instantly at peace and understood experientially that "belief" is a gift from God. It's not an understanding that we can realize without help. It is supernatural and initiated by God (John 6:44). Understanding or comprehending the Scriptures is granted to us by Jesus, the Author and the Finisher of our faith (Hebrews 12:2).

Fortunately, the state of my faith regarding Jesus possibly not being the *only* way, may have been enough for me, but it was not enough for Him. He was not willing to leave me with incomplete faith. Holy Spirit led me on a journey as a professional chaplain where I encountered hundreds of people with different faiths and religious constructs. Through these encounters, God reshaped my faith in all things Jesus, the *only* way to the only living God, the God of the Bible.

I have worked as a professional chaplain in the hospital setting, VA medical centers in two different states, hospice care, and as a corporate chaplain for a Fortune 500 Company. In the pages of this book, I will share spiritual care encounters that were designed by the Father to reveal to me more of the character of God and to aid in the reshaping of my faith in Jesus, the *only* way to God for all of humanity.

Section One
Plot Twist

Chapter 1

Rescue Mission

Leaving my shoes at the door, I entered the new hospice patient's home and convened with him and his family. The new patient and his family were living with his brother and his family. The patient and his family had recently relocated to the United States from India. Their home was being built in the neighborhood across the street. As a hospice chaplain, I was there to conduct a spiritual assessment to determine spiritual needs.

The terminal illness diagnosis was still very new. The patient still looked to be well, the opposite of a terminally ill person, considering what was happening inside his body. He was a picture of health. The family left the decision to him, whether he wanted hospice-provided spiritual support or not, and to my surprise, he wanted chaplain visits.

He identified as Hindu, and in my experience, families who practiced Eastern religions and other non-Christian families typically declined hospice chaplaincy support. They declined because many of them assumed that all chaplains are Christian and that the goal was to convert them to Christianity. Simply, they were not interested in having anyone push religion on them, which is not the goal of professional chaplains.

While professional chaplains are ordained ministers from different faith traditions or organizations (Catholic, Jewish, Hindu, Buddhist, Muslim, Humanist, etc.), they operate differently from an uncertified chaplain or a minister of a faith community working as a chaplain. Professional chaplains do not promote the beliefs of their endorsing denominations or faith traditions. They are trained to support spiritual care seekers in their faith or lack thereof instead of trying to win them to another *without their consent.*

Respecting a person's right to choose what they want to believe or not was new to me considering my Christian background. The concept of me telling people what they ought to believe was challenged in seminary. My assessment of such practices has continued to evolve throughout my professional chaplaincy career, and it has been quite liberating.

Feeling pressured to convert others to Christianity can cause all kinds of anxiety and guilt. Not feeling the pressure to do such felt good to me, but doing nothing initially troubled me. It was also troubling to the Holy Spirit, so He used this encounter to address my concerns, but more importantly, His own concerns about the patient's eternal destiny.

People who practice Eastern religions are also less nostalgic about dying because of their belief in reincarnation, which is when one is reborn immediately following death. Eastern religions are primarily polytheistic and philosophical, but the beauty for them is that there is no supreme God-Being waiting on the other side to whom they will give an account regarding how they lived or not lived.

The concept is that a person is reborn repeatedly until they inherently self-correct whatever prevented them from Nirvana the last time. Nirvana is the end of rebirth, at which point the person goes into a perpetual state of peace or becomes united with a supreme or universal being of sorts. Therefore, there is no fear of death. The person essentially continues to repeat until he/she is perfected by a process of unknown bad behavior elimination.

The patient wanted biweekly visits, so we scheduled for such. I discerned that he was a "good" person, which is how I described it to his family, but it was more than that. I was spiritually drawn to him. There was a connection that I didn't have words for at the time, and he obviously felt it, too, which is why he requested continued chaplain visits. My impression of his goodness was so strong that I verbalized my thoughts, and his family confirmed. Yes, he is a good person; very principled, his sister-in-law reported.

My thoughts towards the patient continued after my visit ended. Doing nothing to "win his soul" was bothering me, so I interceded for him. I reminded Jesus that he was too good of a person to die and go to Hell, which is the destiny of anyone who does not accept Jesus as Savior. No person goes to heaven because they are good or even principled, only because they put their trust in and accept Jesus Christ as Lord and Savior.

John 3:16-17 (ASV): For God so loved the world, that he gave his only begotten Son, that whosoever believeth on him should not perish, but have eternal life. [17] For God sent not the Son into the world to judge the world; but that the world should be saved through him.

I returned for my second visit, and the patient and his family met with me in the family room again. The patient's desire for chaplain visits was surely motivated by the Holy Spirit because the patient didn't have much to say, eventually nothing to say. I discovered at some point after my first visit that the patient accepted his destiny with death. He came to terms with the fact that he would be transitioning to his next life.

Initially, he was not convinced that he had a terminal illness. There had not been any indications that sickness was in his body. There were no warning signs that his organs were being ravished by disease. It did not make sense to him, so he didn't believe that he was dying.

He was a devoted Hindu and had followed all the rules that should have sealed his physical and spiritual well-being in this life and the next. He had strict dietary practices. He exercised daily, practiced meditation, and was considered a good human being. He had done everything prescribed to protect himself from the ills of this earthly experience and the life to come afterwards, but to no avail. The terminal illness had prevailed.

After he fully accepted that his life as he knew it was ending, he stopped speaking. His sister-in-law shared with me that he had a good cry about it and then began emotionally disconnecting. He surrendered to the dying process. He did not just surrender, but he rushed it. He also stopped eating. His sister-in-law inquired about possible tests to determine why he could no longer speak or eat, but it was not a medical condition. The patient was not afraid of death, so if his life was to end, he was ready to surrender to the process.

The patient believed in reincarnation and was confident that his life had been well lived. According to his belief, rebirth was based on how the adherent lived the previous life, and if the adherent lived well enough, there would be a release and no further need for rebirth, Nirvana. The suffering of living in this world would be over. The patient had full expectations that this was his destiny. He was at peace with his passing and felt no desire to delay it.

I continued my visits, but my time was primarily spent with his sister-in-law. Her adherence to Hinduism had led her towards a more informed and elevated version of the religion, and she shared her journey with me. I often became a student in my chaplain encounters, especially when people of other faiths were involved. I didn't know it then, but my chaplain encounters were primarily case studies. Jesus was essentially undoing what had been done to me in seminary.

Philippians 1:6 (ASV): being confident of this very thing, that he who began a good work in you will perfect it until the day of Jesus Christ:

Many of these encounters were juxtapositions of salvation through Jesus and the ambiguous endgame for some of the mainstream religions. I was genuinely curious and receptive to other ways of believing. My purpose for going to seminary was to expand my mind, and my mind was indeed stretched.

A huge difference between who I was when I started seminary and who I became was that I was at least receptive to the possibility of there being something more to the other religions. Of course, Jesus remains the *only* way for me, but maybe there was something there with the others, so I gave space to my curiosity.

The patient's sister-in-law shared with me her journey to this deeper awakening and other details about her journey. She credited her guru for getting her through hard times, and I was never tempted to try to take her faith from her. She had her journey, and I had mine. I met her where she was, which was in the arms of Jesus, and I left her there.

Jesus carried her through those hard times, whether she gives Him credit for it or not. Because of His dying love for all of humanity, the Holy Spirit will provide merciful interventions and comfort regardless of our religious constructs because that is what love does. Unconditional love is not contingent upon the response of the beneficiary.

Romans 5:8 (WEB): *But God commends his own love toward us, in that while we were yet sinners, Christ died for us.*

Besides, I was sent for her dying brother-in-law, I discovered, although, in the end, I only saw him for a few minutes during each visit, long enough to say "hi." By the end of my time with the family, the patient was bedbound. He spent his last days upstairs in bed. I was allowed upstairs, but I was never allowed to spend time alone with the patient. When I went upstairs to his room, the whole family would also stop what they were doing and join us.

I have been told by at least two New Age types that Christian Believers have some sort of glow around us that is discernable by the clairvoyant types. I heard someone else say that all true Believers have a discernible light within but that the brightness of the light is based on the person's level of submission or obedience to the Holy Spirit. While some have flickers of light, others blazing infernos, and the remaining somewhere in between.

Also, in my experience, people of other faiths have more awareness of the spiritual world than Christians. I don't know what they saw in or about me, but they saw something because they acted as guards over the patient's soul. The family members were all very nice, but they did not trust me alone with the patient.

Essentially, I was trespassing. The home was a literal altar to the Hindu gods. There was a huge altar erected to them in the living room, complete with food sacrifices and other paraphernalia laid out for them. I imagine that even a flicker of light is very bright amidst this kind of spiritual darkness.

The last time I visited the home of this family the primary caregiver had an emergency, so she was not available for our usual time together. She directed me upstairs to spend time with the patient instead. Utterly surprised, I went upstairs and entered the patient's room. I felt an urgency, so I leaned into it. I saw the patient's wife sitting on the floor in the hallway folding clothes, but she did not drop what she was doing to join us, and nor did anyone else. The others weren't home on this day.

The patient was lying awake in bed. He was down to about fifty pounds or less. His face was sunken. His eyes had dark circles around them. They were bulging and filled with fright. His eyes met with mine and followed me as I entered the room. I greeted him as I approached the bed.

In my experience of hospice chaplaincy, dying patients often have supernatural experiences at the end of life, including having glimpses of their next destination, as well as the people or beings that inhabit such places. I was curious to know if the patient had experienced such, so I asked him. I walked into the room, asking the patient two questions, had he seen where he was going, and did he like it? He did not speak with his mouth, but he had his wits about him. He responded with a nod for "yes" and a head shake for "no." He had a glimpse of where he was going, and he did NOT like it.

Of course, I was as shocked as you are right now, so I asked the same questions again, but I got right up in his face to be sure that I understood what he was communicating to me. I also didn't want to alert anyone. He answered the same.

The Bible is very clear regarding the destiny of those who do not accept Jesus as Lord and Savior and His salvation plan, but it is very different when it is confirmed in real-time. Something was waiting for the patient on the other side, but it wasn't good. He was not heading to Nirvana, and he was disturbed by the revelation.

I then asked him if he was okay with me telling him about my faith and, afterwards, if he wanted me to pray a salvation prayer with him where he'd meet Jesus instead of what he saw previously. He responded again with nods for "yes" and "yes". I held his hand and prayed with him while he nodded in agreement to his decision to put his trust in Jesus. This entire encounter probably took less than ten minutes. Jesus gave this faithful Hindu man a glimpse of his afterlife and an option to change course, and he took the out.

During this encounter, his wife came to the doorway but did not enter the room or say anything. I felt her presence, but I did not look back or acknowledge her. She did not interrupt my visit by entering the room as she had with the others all the other times before. Fortunately, her English was not as good, so she possibly didn't understand what we spoke about. On the other hand, as a wife, she knew better than anyone that her husband had been spooked by something unexpected, so she gave me time alone with him. Nirvana was not awaiting his arrival as they both had expected.

I felt an urgency to leave immediately after we prayed. I hurried downstairs, slipped back into my shoes, and hurried to my car. I normally sat in the driveway to enter notes about my visit, but there wasn't time for that on this day. I understood that this would not be good news for the rest of the family. It was a betrayal to them, but I couldn't worry about that. Jesus had tag-teamed me into the situation, and that was that. The patient transitioned a few days later, but I am confident that I will see him again.

In the meantime, I called to extend my condolences and offered the family grief support for up to one year, as mandated by the Centers of Medicare and Medicaid Services, but his brother declined. I knew from his tone that the patient or his wife had shared the patient's salvation experience with Jesus with the family.

His brother seemed proud to report that he had officiated the patient's *Hindu-styled* funeral, which was appropriate. Funerals are for the left behind, not dearly departed saints. My spiritual care for this family ended, but my confidence in Jesus being the *only* way for all of humanity was sealed.

John 14:6 (WEB): Jesus said to him, "I am the way, the truth, and the life. No one comes to the Father, except through me.

I also no longer struggled with whether I should or should not try to convert people to Christianity. I realized that Jesus was already working these cases long before I was invited into the situation and that He would tag me in if or when He wanted to, and I would recognize when He did so. The Holy Spirit had lured this patient to the United States from India, where he discovered he had a terminal illness, signed up for hospice care, was introduced to Jesus, and then transitioned to be with Him for all of eternity.

John 6:44 (WEB): No one can come to me unless the Father who sent me draws him; and I will raise him up in the last day.

The Father's love had tracked this patient since birth, and when the time was right, Jesus revealed Himself or enough of something otherworldly to cause pause for this patient. I was merely tagged in on the backend for the purpose of confirming to me that Father is the One who does the drawing. I was never again anxious about trying to find a way to force Jesus on people or into the conversation. Holy Spirit will lead the way because He has already prepped the situation.

Jesus simply loves every individual too much to leave His salvation plan exclusively to humans. He is unwilling to gamble over someone's soul like that. God is ALWAYS at work seeking to draw unbelievers to Himself. He merely uses others if or when we are in place to catch the fish that He throws into our hands. Of course, all my spiritual care encounters did not end this way. Some people boldly rejected the *only* Way.

POW! (Pearls of Wisdom): Good people don't go to heaven; only those who accept Jesus as Savior do.

Chapter 2

Surprised by Death

I drove past the chicken farm on my way up the long driveway to the large white house at the top of the hill. The hospice patient's adult daughter greeted me at the door and escorted me to the patient's room. He was resting in a sunroom that overlooked his large property. The view was very calming. I had weekly scheduled visits with him. This wasn't my first visit, but it would be the last.

The patient was in his late seventies and still a very active businessman prior to the terminal illness. Getting back to his several businesses was his motivation for getting well. He was no longer able to walk nor take care of his daily needs due to his debilitating illness, but he was committed to resolving his mobility issues. A physical therapist was among the gang of professionals who brought his care to his home throughout the week. His illness was terminal, but he didn't believe that he was dying. He had full expectations that he would fully recover and resume his life as it was before.

One of the conditions of hospice care is that the patient or his/her proxy agrees to cease emergency room visits and other life-saving measures in relationship to the hospice-diagnosed terminal illness. Most patients had a Do Not Resuscitate form on file, while others vehemently refused. Instead of the patient going to the ER, the hospice nurse comes to the home and takes care of the needs. This patient did not follow those rules.

He went back and forth to the ER for various issues in the end, which meant that he had to end his contract with hospice care while at the hospital and then re-enroll when he was discharged.

He had spent the previous weekend in the hospital. He returned home and came back to hospice care the day before my visit.

The patient's sister, who was his primary caregiver, was a Christian, so she was committed to stuffing Jesus into him, whether he wanted Him or not. He described her as the fiery, no-nonsense type, likening her to one of the television judges. As a Christian minister, she expected me to do the same, but it wasn't my role to push in this way. Unlike with hospital patients, my approach with hospice patients was very different.

For the most part, my chaplain visits with hospital patients could be categorized as one-night stands. There wasn't always time to develop relationships. I didn't know if they would still be in the hospital the next day or by the time I returned to them. Patients were in and out more quickly, so I often got straight to the point regarding their spirituality and how their beliefs informed their response to sickness. Hospice chaplaincy was very different.

Hospice patients are in hospice care because medical professionals have determined that they will die within six months if their terminal illness progresses in the manner that is anticipated. Different people process this information differently. Some take heed and plan accordingly, while others shut down spiritually. They completely reject meaningful conversations about their spirituality and the end-of-life journey, so it can be a much slower process.

Therefore, I appreciated his sister's aggressive approach because it at least gave me a quicker way into his spirituality. I got right to the point and used his sister's insistence as an excuse for bringing the issue up sooner. I broached the subject with the patient during my first visit, several weeks earlier.

He shared that he had grown up loving Jesus as a Christian Believer. He was a minister of music as a young adult, eventually leading a traveling Christian band, but his young wife shut his ministry down. She did not approve so he gave it all up, including Jesus. He became a businessman instead.

Matthew 6:24 (WEB): "No one can serve two masters, for either he will hate the one and love the other, or else he will be devoted to one and despise the other. You can't serve both God and Mammon.

He had plans of returning to Jesus one day, but not yet. He was still looking forward to making his businesses even more successful. In retrospect, I don't know why he felt he had to choose between Jesus and business. It is quite possible to do both well, unless he had to compromise his integrity in business. I wish I had explored it further.

Revelation 3:15-20 (WEB): "I know your works, that you are neither cold nor hot. I wish you were cold or hot. [16] So, because you are lukewarm, and neither hot nor cold, I will vomit you out of my mouth. [17] Because you say, 'I am rich, and have gotten riches, and have need of nothing,' and don't know that you are the wretched one, miserable, poor, blind, and naked; [18] I counsel you to buy from me gold refined by fire, that you may become rich; and white garments, that you may clothe yourself, and that the shame of your nakedness may not be revealed; and eye salve to anoint your eyes, that you may see. [19] As many as I love, I reprove and chasten. Be zealous therefore, and repent. [20] Behold, I stand at the door and knock. If anyone hears my voice and opens the door, then I will come in to him and will dine with him, and he with me.

At least he had enough reverence for Abba to understand that he couldn't do both if indeed his business dealings were less than honorable. He chose his side and Abba respects that. When I asked him about his relationship with God, he shared that he was not ready to reconcile his relationship, so I respectfully left it alone. We spent the time talking about random other things.

This patient's last hospital visit alarmed his family, so they were gathering at his house. They believed that the end was near for him. I was there to see him for the same reason. While I was alone in the sunroom with him, the doorbell rang several times as new guests arrived to see him. After hearing the buzz of the crowd grow louder, the patient finally asked with a bit of frustration in his voice, why were all the people coming to the house. Surprised, I told him that they were coming to see him because they thought he was going to die soon.

My words stunned him. He was visibly shaken, trembling. He had ignored or rejected the signs that death was near to him. He was determined to go back to his business, and that was all he considered. Despite his declining health, he didn't believe that death was near to him.

Luke 12:20-21 (WEB): "But God said to him, 'You foolish one, tonight your soul is required of you. The things which you have prepared—whose will they be?' [21] *So is he who lays up treasure for himself, and is not rich toward God."*

I waited in silence for him to calm himself. He sat there in shock for several minutes. I eventually broke the silence and asked him if he wanted time alone to reconsider reconciling his relationship with Jesus sooner rather than later. He responded, "Yes," so I left him alone to think about it.

I joined his family members, who were gathered in the living room. I could feel the anxiety in the room when I entered. They were a churchgoing family, but they were scared. They didn't know how to respond to the situation. He was the wealthy patriarch of the family, Big Poppa. He was seemingly the only one of them who was no longer churchgoing. I mentioned to them that he was reconsidering a decision to reconcile with Jesus Christ and invited them to pray with me for him.

To my surprise, fear identified himself and very spiritedly commanded that I "leave him be!" His sister's response caught me off guard. She was the one pressuring him about his relationship with Jesus. I was surprised because only the devil gets mad when a person is considering reconciling with Jesus, so I understood that it wasn't her speaking. This chaplain encounter took place later in my chaplain career, so I had encountered this sort of thing before.

2 Timothy 1:7 (WEB): For God didn't give us a spirit of fear, but of power, love, and self-control.

Thankfully, this was the extent of the outburst. We all joined hands, prayed for the patient, and I returned to the patient in the other room without further incident. In retrospect, I considered that the patient's sister had feelings regarding me being the person in place to facilitate his reconciliation with Jesus. Soul "winning" is a competitive sport in some religious circles. It is a bragging right for folks who have been charged by their pastors with this call. She had nurtured that seed for years and now there was someone else there to witness the manifestation of her work.

1 Corinthians 3:6-8 (WEB): I planted. Apollos watered. But God gave the increase. ⁷ So then neither he who plants is anything, nor he who waters, but God who gives the increase. ⁸ Now he who plants and he who waters are the same, but each will receive his own reward according to his own labor.

The patient was still stunned but sober when I returned to him. He decided that he wanted to invite Jesus back into his heart. He reconciled his relationship with Jesus. We prayed together, and shortly afterwards, I ended my visit. He died a few days later.

I was often surprised by the organic connection between myself and the most unlikely patients, including this one. The barriers (race, socioeconomic status, gender, age, religion) that separate us weren't felt in these instances. The pairings were always completely unexpected.

This patient and I would have never had a reason to exchange phone numbers in the grocery store or in line at the DMV. In essence, this was Jesus' way of demonstrating that He is the One setting up these unlikely relationships, but exclusively for His salvation purposes.

POW! (Pearls of Wisdom): Death doesn't always wait for us to plan or to get ready for it.

Chapter 3

Rerouted

The wife of the new hospice patient hobbled to the door and invited me into their home. She was recovering from an ankle injury incurred during a recent Pickle Ball tournament. She escorted me to the living room, where we were joined by the couple's adult son. The patient was upstairs. They identified themselves as Christian Believers and members of a nearby Methodist church where the patient was a deacon.

I spoke with the patient's wife and adult son for at least an hour, but to my surprise they did not schedule additional chaplain visits. I was also not invited to meet the patient during my visit. We had a great conversation, but I wasn't invited back. At this point in my hospice chaplaincy career, I understood that the caregivers were the gatekeepers.

They decided if the patient would receive spiritual support from the hospice chaplain, and the decision rarely had anything to do with the patient's spiritual need or desire for the service. The dying patient was at the mercy of the primary caregiver, and so was I, in terms of being granted additional visits. In many ways, my spiritual assessment visits were auditions and sometimes I didn't get through.

The reasons for caregivers declining chaplain services ranged from lack of interest in spirituality, caregivers being too busy or not seeing value in the service to a plethora of other known and unknown reasons, including someone being angry with God because God allowed the illness.

Also, at this point in my chaplain career, I had noticed a pattern with Christian patients or their families, those who had dedicated their lives to Christian service. They seemingly felt

21

entitled to a trouble-free life in exchange for their rendered service to Jesus. They became angry when things didn't work out according to their health expectations. Terminal illness was an insult to them. Of course, no one verbally disclosed these thoughts and feelings of anger and betrayal, but the anger manifested in different ways.

This family fit the profile, but since I was not being invited back, I did not have days, weeks, or months to spare. Discerning that my visit was coming to an end without an invitation to return, I asked the patient's wife what seemed to have been a staggering question. I asked her if either she or the patient were angry with God for allowing the illness. This had been the Holy Spirit prompting me because it was unusual for me to be that direct in these situations.

With a look of bewilderment on her face, the patient's wife responded with a soft "no". The question triggered her, but she had no further comments. Shortly afterwards, I ended my visit with no appointment to return. I moved on to the next family.

A few days later, I received a call from the hospice nurse. She requested a chaplain visit on behalf of this family. The patient's wife had not requested the visit. The patient was actively transitioning, but his transition was stalled. The hospice nurse did not want to leave the patient's wife alone, so she asked me to come over to sit with her as the patient completed his transition.

The patient's transition was taking longer than usual due to suspected spiritual distress, some unresolved issue that was preventing the patient from peacefully completing the transitioning process. This distress can be caused by an array of different reasons, including waiting to see a particular family member, waiting for loved ones to be at peace with them dying, fear of death, and other reasons.

In those times, the hospice team would educate the caregiver or family on possible interventions to relieve the distress. Families are encouraged to try to identify the source of the distress and, if possible, meet the unmet needs of the dying patient. The nurse seemingly educated the patient's wife on some interventions, called and asked me to come over, and left the home.

When I arrived the patient's wife was employing some of the interventions. Among other things, she was assuring the patient that she would be okay when he died. This was likely a concern for the patient. He was much older than his wife. She seemed more like a daughter than a wife. She was childlike in many ways, also emotionally and mentally fragile.

She was crying hysterically, beating the patient in his chest, and pleading with him to go when I arrived. Amid her beating and sobbing, she mentioned that the patient had disclosed feelings of anger towards God regarding the terminal illness and his unjustified hospice death sentence. She disclosed that she had asked him about it after I inquired about it during my first visit.

After I heard this, I understood what was happening, so I inserted myself into the situation. I knelt and spoke to the patient directly. He was unresponsive. His eyes were half open and glazed over, and he had labored breathing. I spoke to him about his anger towards Jesus and the implications of trying to enter the Father's presence with anger towards Him.

Exodus 3:3-5 (WEB): Moses said, "I will go now, and see this great sight, why the bush is not burned."⁴ When Yahweh saw that he came over to see, God called to him out of the middle of the bush, and said, "Moses! Moses!" He said, "Here I am." ⁵ He said, "Don't come close. Take off your sandals, for the place you are standing on is holy ground."

A veteran that I served at a VA medical center, once told me that with all the trouble going on in the world, he just didn't believe that God was doing a good job running the world. His sweet elderly mother literally clutched her pearls. She was shocked that the boy that she had taken to Sunday school throughout his childhood would say such blasphemous things about the Creator of the universe.

Abba, in His mercy, tolerates a lot of foolishness from humankind. He remembers that we are dust. Therefore, this hospice patient's delayed or stalled transition was more than likely Abba's mercy, otherwise the patient would have been allowed to transition without an opportunity to repent.

Psalm 103:14 (WEB): For he knows how we are made. He remembers that we are dust.

Apparently, death is not one of those "anything goes" situations that Jesus is willing to overlook. There is a way to go into eternity, the presence of Holy God, and apparently, with an angry spirit or foul attitude is not the way.

The patient was already unresponsive, unable to physically and verbally respond. I understood that he was still consciously trapped in his body, so I spoke to him, accordingly, encouraging him to let go of his anger. This was surely one of those tag-team situations. Jesus led me to explain to the patient that adjustments in his attitude had to be made for him to transition into the place that has been prepared for those who love God. I then prayed with the patient and ended my visit, confident that he had also heard with his spiritual ears. A different hospice nurse had arrived by this time.

The patient's wife called me shortly after I left their home and reported that the patient had passed over. She was convinced that he was able to peacefully transition after he settled his issue of anger with Abba, and I believe the same.

Ephesians 4:26-27 (WEB): "Be angry, and don't sin." Don't let the sun go down on your wrath, [27] and don't give place to the devil.

It was an act of love and a demonstration of the Father's mercy. The patient was being spared from the devastation and destruction that awaited him if he transitioned without forsaking the spirit of anger, thereby resolving the issue of his heart. He was physically unresponsive to human stimulation, but his spirit was still in his body with the ability to choose or reject reconciliation with Jesus Christ.

Every person who puts their trust in Jesus is saved and heaven bound as we walk out the sanctification process. Unfortunately, sin is still a factor in the life of Christian Believers, but confession is the Believer's antidote for each continued bout with it. I use the word 'bout' because there is an expectation that the born-again Believer, with the Holy Spirit's help, ceases to *practice* sin and keeps himself/herself clean from a *lifestyle* of sin.

1 John 1:9 (ASV): If we confess our sins, he is faithful and righteous to forgive us our sins, and to cleanse us from all unrighteousness.

At the same time, individual slipups are inevitable and are consequences of being broken people living in a broken world. Therefore, confession is a powerful gift extended to Christians, and it clears the way to forgiveness and cleansing from all unrighteousness as sinful behaviors continue to pop up. Confession enables Believers to be restored and to remain in right standing with Jesus, after bouts of sin creep in. Those who continue to unapologetically *practice* sin thereby having a lifestyle of sin are deceived and are not children of God.

I am often befuddled by folks who proudly and unapologetically live in known biblical sin, but do not seek nor are interested in deliverance from that sin while claiming to be

Christians. This is not the will of God. We are to be active participants in our individual sanctification processes, not denying the need for such. Among other things, this lifestyle of intentional sinning is evidence that the person is not partnered with the Holy Spirit in the reading of the Holy Scriptures.

When we read the Bible, it also reads us. It's alive and relevant for every generation. I have read the Bible from cover to cover more than once, but I am sometimes shocked when new sinful aspects of my heart are revealed to me in Scripture, as if I never saw it in the Bible before.

It is possible that the newly revealed sinfulness was not a problem for me the last time I read the verses, or that I had too many other issues to work out before Holy Spirit wanted to hit me with a new one. The revelation of our personal sinfulness can be overwhelming, so Jesus is merciful. Abba is not expecting perfection from us at this point, only active engagement in the sanctification process. The Bible, the word of God is our help.

Hebrews 4:12 (ASV): For the word of God is living, and active, and sharper than any two-edged sword, and piercing even to the dividing of soul and spirit, of both joints and marrow, and quick to discern the thoughts and intents of the heart.

Many of us have our favorite Scriptures, books of the Bible, or even our favorite of the two testaments. I personally like the Old Testament more, so I circle there more. However, I was recently on a spiritual fast with some other folks, and we were challenged to read through the New Testament in twenty-one days, about thirteen chapters a day.

For some reason, Jesus' words in the Gospels hit me differently. I discerned an urgency that I had not felt before; more of a "Get it together, now!" sound to it. What's interesting is that the following Sunday, my pastor said the same thing regarding his heightened awareness of the potency of Jesus's words during his reading of the New Testament during the church-wide fast. My point simply is that reading the Bible positions us to hear God's heart and His specific instructions to us as individuals, at the time that we need His direction.

Romans 6:1-4 (ASV): What shall we say then? Shall we continue in sin, that grace may abound? [2] God forbid. We who died to sin, how shall we any longer live therein? [3] Or are ye ignorant that all we who were baptized into Christ Jesus were baptized into his death? [4] We were buried therefore with him through baptism into death: that like as Christ was raised from the dead through the glory of the Father, so we also might walk in newness of life.

The hospice patient was at odds with Jesus. He had repeatedly allowed the sun to go down on his anger, so he was stuck. An angry person cannot get into heaven for stated reasons, but also because of the risk of contamination. The Father will not allow that again (Rev 12). This patient had a change of heart, laid down his anger and was granted access and a peaceful transition.

POW! (Pearls of Wisdom): Fix your heart. You can't go to the Father's house angry with Him.

Chapter 4

Unpopular Pardons

I entered the Veterans Affairs Medical Center hospital room of a veteran who had served our country in the Vietnam War. I was there to assess his spiritual needs. I loved working with the veterans because they understood and appreciated the role of chaplains more than most.

In my experience, they were transparent and direct communicators. They can handle uncomfortable conversations and often introduce them. The raw exchanges were more in-line with my preferred style of communication. There was no pretense, and I rarely had to figure out what they were communicating to me. I also appreciated the fact that I didn't have to fight them for the opportunity to serve them. They practiced full disclosure, but this veteran's transparency was on a different level.

I initiated storytelling, and he began telling me his story. Seconds into his story, he began confessing his past sins of racism. He detailed his discriminatory practices against Black Americans when he worked as a property manager after being discharged from military service years earlier. I initially challenged him regarding his need to disclose such things to me, a Black American woman, but I determined that he meant no disrespect. I realized that my presence had triggered him. He saw me and remembered the folks that looked like me whom he had discriminated against years earlier.

1 John 4:20-21 (WEB): If a man says, "I love God," and hates his brother, he is a liar; for he who doesn't love his brother whom he has seen, how can he love God whom he has not seen? [21] This commandment we have from him, that he who loves God should also love his brother.

He spoke of his past indiscretions and it seemed to be a spiritual cleansing of sorts, so I resisted the urge to feel offended. It just wasn't about me. He paused from his storytelling periodically and wept. I asked probing questions, he disclosed more details and wept more until he got it all out. He eventually pulled himself together, we talked more, and then I ended my visit feeling satisfied that I had served him well.

As a professional chaplain, more than ninety-five percent of my spiritual care encounters have been with people of a different race than me. I have primarily worked in rural areas and areas where there weren't many Black Americans. The locals just didn't have real-life or meaningful contact with Black Americans, so biases were prevalent.

Many had seemingly opted to exclusively believe the negative images shown on the evening news. Therefore, many of God's people didn't know they had these biases until I showed up in their hospital rooms, homes, or workspaces as a minister of the Jesus that they claimed to know and love. My presence often triggered some racially charged reactions.

The worst involved a different Vietnam veteran who insisted on debating me regarding his support of the public use of the "n" word. He insisted that he really didn't know why it was such a big deal. He gave up his position when I asked him if he was also in support of the public use of the derogatory "c" word that's used for White Americans.

My visit with him eventually came to a civilized end, but before I could leave the room, he extended his hand for a handshake. He gave me one of those two-handed handshakes, where he cupped my hand between his. I still remember how warm and soft his hands were. With a smile on his face, he leaned closer to me and whispered in my ear that I was just a "n" and that's all I was. He said it twice, but he used the actual word.

My visit with him had gone well until he discovered that I had a master's degree from a school that had a reputation that he respected. He discovered such when he couldn't resist the urge to inquire about my chaplain credentials. This veteran wanted to injure me with his words because something had obviously gone wrong in his life.

My presence had also triggered him, but his response was opposite that of the first veteran. His racism had been cultivated since childhood in rural small-town, USA. Unfortunately, I was familiar with such settings. I was raised in the city of Atlanta, but I relocated to such a town in my forties.

After graduating seminary, I moved away from Metro-Atlanta to a small town for my first hospice chaplain job. I was initially concerned about how I would be received as a Black American female chaplain in this area, but my concerns were initially put to rest. Many of the families on hospice care had hired help in their homes to assist with the needs of the hospice patients and to also perform other household duties. These women were mostly Black Americans, so there was at least a level of familiarity.

Black American women have a complicated history with White American families. Black American women began their American journey cleaning their homes, cooking their food, washing their clothes, taking care of their children, and keeping their secrets. Unfortunately, many White Americans cannot accept Black Americans outside of those roles. This became apparent to me in this small town. There was a clear line of demarcation between the races, but it was probably more apparent to me, as an outsider, than to the Black folks who lived and were raised there.

I discovered that my ministry was not wholly received in the same way as the offerings of these women, but only because I wasn't cleaning their homes, cooking their food, washing their clothes, and taking care of their children. Unfortunately, I found this to be a reality across the spectrum of my chaplain career. My spiritual care ministry was not wholly accepted by those who needed me to be subordinate to them, but that wasn't the case with the first veteran. He was genuinely trying to work out his salvation.

Philippians 2:12 (WEB): So then, my beloved, even as you have always obeyed, not only in my presence, but now much more in my absence, work out your own salvation with fear and trembling.

God's children are ashamed when Holy Spirit brings awareness to them regarding this issue. The children of God are grateful for the exposure, so they confront and repent from such, which is essentially, all the Father wants, a changed heart. Jesus' goal is to heal, not to shame anyone just for the sake of shaming.

Years after this encounter, I was working with a hospice patient who also had an issue of racism. I arrived at her house, and she did not conceal her irritation. I was an hour late, she said. I was not. I didn't agree with her, but I didn't argue with her. I later learned that she had me confused with our hospice social worker, the other brown person on our hospice team. On the other hand, it wasn't unusual for terminally ill patients to be confused due to illness or medications, but that wasn't it in this case. There were other indicators. Her anger was over the top for the situation. I soon discovered that her reaction had little to do with punctuality. She was triggered by the color of my skin.

I don't know if this new hospice patient had been one of the patients who requested such, but some of the families in her area asked the hospice company to ensure that Black Americans were not assigned to provide hospice care to their families. Of course, the parent company officially rejected the business of those with such requests, but not so much in the local offices. I was given the "opportunity" to transfer to a different office shortly after questioning the handling of such requests.

I continued with my spiritual assessment and learned that this new patient was a Christian. Her reaction to me might have even caught her by surprise. As a Christian, she possibly felt the conviction of the Holy Spirit regarding her racist reaction to me but struggled to control it.

She was in her eighties. She lived in the mountains. Her log cabin styled home was built and passed down by previous generations. It was built during a time when I, as a Black American woman, could not make eye contact with her without consequence. In contrast, I was sitting on her couch, and not cleaning her home, cooking her food, washing her clothes, and taking care of her dogs. I also wasn't there to entertain her. This was seemingly too much reality for her to process in the moments of my time with her.

There were also instances when I understood that some of my White American patients were genuinely confused and upset that Jesus had allowed terminal illness to invade their life, while I, as a Black American and descendant of African slaves, still had my health. They viewed themselves as of a superior race, more precious in the Father's sight. My wellness in view of their terminal illness was an injustice to them. I suspect that this was the case with this patient.

She tried to settle herself, but she was having a hard time. She wasn't doing anything outrageous, but her indignation was obvious. I wasn't altogether surprised that she was racist. I was surprised that she identified as a Christian. I am still somewhat baffled by that, a racist Christian.

Another responsibility I had as a chaplain was to attend and officiate funerals and memorial services of patients or team members if there was a need or request. I was often the only Black

American in attendance, and I was primarily invisible to the other ministers of the Gospel of Jesus Christ. Some pastors avoided eye contact, while others were filled with indignation that I had the nerve to answer my "call". They were intentional in their attempts to communicate to me that I did not belong.

1 John 3:14-16 (WEB): We know that we have passed out of death into life, because we love the brothers. He who doesn't love his brother remains in death. [15] Whoever hates his brother is a murderer, and you know that no murderer has eternal life remaining in him. [16] By this we know love, because he laid down his life for us. And we ought to lay down our lives for the brothers.

As I write about some of these encounters, I consider why I wasn't more offended than I seemingly could have been at the time and then I remember. Initially I was just glad that Jesus found me worthy of service to Him, thereby calling me off the church building bench and putting me in the game. I developed more skill and had more grace for marketplace ministry.

I recall providing spiritual care to a racially aggressive veteran whom I also served at a VA Medical Center. He was openly filled with indignation towards anyone who didn't look like him. He was not shy regarding his thoughts about the VA's practice of hiring such people. I was called to the scene by the nursing staff in hopes that a chaplain might have success with calming down this veteran.

The staff didn't anticipate that the on-call chaplain would be a Black American woman. Fortunately, the veteran was not as cantankerous with me. Good religious racist folk are pious enough to pretend with the chaplain, and I was good with that. As an introvert and a primarily task-oriented person, I also had to pretend, a lot.

This veteran was loud and proud of his crazy. During one of his rants, his phone rung and he calmed down immediately when he saw that it was his fiancé calling. He did not want her to witness his crazy on this level. From that day forward, I used conversation about his fiancé as kryptonite. He was a different person when he spoke about her.

Unfortunately, his health took a nosedive, and he received a prognosis of less than a few days to live. Within a few days I officiated his hospital bedside wedding, and then the eulogy at his funeral. The look on the faces of his family and friends who attended these services was priceless.

Everyone knew him to be racist because he was loud and proud about it, but Jesus changed his heart in his last days. He asked a Black American woman to officiate his wedding, and his new wife asked me to officiate and to eulogize him at his funeral. My involvement in his life was good for him. Experiencing me likely lessened the shock of him getting to heaven and seeing it also filled with others who looked like me. Hopefully, this hospice patient was also able to transform herself.

I finally figured out that by God's design, I was there to trigger awareness with this new hospice patient. This is the love of the Father and His commitment to purify His children. Holy Spirit wanted to make her aware of what was in her heart, in hopes that she would repent. Heaven is not the place for racially hateful people.

This patient didn't schedule more chaplain visits. She passed away a few days later, and to my surprise, her transition was what is referred to in hospice care as a "good death". Anyone who has worked in a profession where they witness a lot of death, understands that people die differently. It is not always a peaceful transition, and I considered that maybe this patient's transition would not be a peaceful one because of the race-based hate that was seemingly lodged in her soul.

Some of these transitioning episodes were like a fright night, with disturbing happenings, but that was not the case with this patient. She transitioned peacefully and without incident, teaching me something very important about the character of the Father. His ways are not our ways. He "feels" what we feel, but he does not "think" the same about these things as we do. His thoughts and ways are higher than ours. Redemption is His desired goal for all sinners.

Isaiah 55:8-9 (ASV): For my thoughts are not your thoughts, neither are your ways my ways, saith Jehovah. [9] For as the heavens are higher than the earth, so are my ways higher than your ways, and my thoughts than your thoughts.

Hell was created for the devil and his angels, not human beings. Jesus is not willing that any should perish, not even repentant child molesters, likely the most reviled of sinners, in the minds of human beings. I once provided spiritual care to an eighty-year-old hospice patient who was convicted of sexually assaulting his grandson.

He was in hospice care enduring terminal illness, but also on house arrest. The terminal illness diagnosis and his age had kept him out of prison. He wore a monitoring bracelet on his ankle until the day of his death. His son, the father of the molested child, also suspected that there were more victims, including the youth at their church, neighbors, and friends. The patient was a youth pastor for years and had worked with children throughout his life.

The patient never accused his grandchild of lying, only that he didn't remember the crimes. None of us want to remember or to think about our worst deeds or sins in life. He submitted that whatever his grandchild said he did was the truth. This same patient once asked me if I believed Jesus could or would forgive a child molester and allow them into heaven. My answer is "yes".

I discovered that Jesus is radical in his plight to forgive all repentant sinners. It turns out that racism and not even sexual assault against a child are unpardonable sins for those who repent and accept Jesus' gift of salvation. Abba is not willing that any should perish.

2 Peter 3:9 (WEB): The Lord is not slow concerning his promise, as some count slowness; but he is patient with us, not wishing that anyone should perish, but that all should come to repentance.

For reasons like this, I learned to see even illness as a blessing. Long-term illness awards time for personal and meaningful reflection that can lead to repentance and a changed heart. God tarries long and appeals to humankind until the very end in hopes of pardoning personal sin, but only if the offender is willing to address it, as this patient likely did.

POW! (Pearls of Wisdom): All sinners are given the opportunity to repent and to reboot their hearts.

Section Two
Inconvenient Truth

Chapter 5

Little God

The husband of the new hospice patient opened the door to their home and invited me inside. I was there to conduct a spiritual assessment. The couple had signed up for hospice care later rather than sooner. Many families refuse hospice care because accepting the care makes the terminal illness and impending death more real. This was the case in this situation. The patient was not ready to surrender to death or the process that was taking her there. Hospice care was called because her husband needed and wanted help taking care of her. He was her sole caregiver.

The rest of the hospice team was with the patient upstairs when I arrived, so the patient's husband escorted me to his office, where he filled me in on the patient's spiritual history. He disclosed that he was an atheist but that the patient had been raised Catholic, so he requested a Catholic priest to come over and perform last rites. I had the contact information for a Catholic priest that I often called on, but I wanted to speak with the patient directly to confirm her wishes. It was not unusual for family or friends to assign to patients a religion that they did not ascribe to.

Confirming the spirituality of choice with the patients was my way of protecting their right to make decisions about their spirituality if they could. Secondly, it gave me an opportunity to explore with them how their religion, spirituality, or lack thereof informed their response to terminal illness. Thirdly, it was also my way of prompting patients to verbally identify their spiritually. It is beneficial for a person to hear out loud, and from their own lips what they believe. Essentially, I became a witness in these situations. Our words will testify for, or against us and they are recorded in eternity.

Matthew 12:36-37 (WEB): I tell you that every idle word that men speak, they will give account of it in the day of judgment. [37] For by your words you will be justified, and by your words you will be condemned."

I became a Christian Believer in my mid-twenties. I eventually asked Jesus why He didn't appeal to me earlier in my life and he eventually answered me by replaying for me the times that He had. In this case, I was joining the roaster of people that Jesus sent to this patient, but I was also testifying on my own behalf. All Christian Believers will stand before the Judgment Seat of Christ.

2 Corinthians 5:9-10 (KJV): Wherefore we labour, that, whether present or absent, we may be accepted of him. [10] For we must all appear before the judgment seat of Christ; that every one may receive the things done in his body, according to that he hath done, whether it be good or bad.

The patient's husband shared that he had gravitated towards atheism in college and more during his military career, but that he had started out as a Christian. He had been raised Southern Baptist and went through confirmation as a youth. He seemed to have turned his back on Jesus after the accidental and unexpected drowning of the daughter that he shared with his first wife. After speaking to him that afternoon, it was clear to me that he wasn't really an atheist. He was disappointed.

I met with the patient after the hospice nurse completed his evaluation. I was introduced to her, and I felt immediate sorrow for her. She was in the early stages of transitioning. She rejected this reality, but her body was proceeding without her consent.

Transitioning is a term used in hospice care to describe the process that many patients go through before the actual death occurs. Transitioning entails gradual disengagement from this world while looking into the next. The process is physical but also spiritual and social. Over time, the person has progressively less interest and attachment to this world. The closer the person gets to death, the more they disengage from this world in various ways, but this wasn't the case with this patient. When I met her, she was still very much attached to this world. She was distracted by random worldly things, primarily things associated with a future with her husband.

She was twenty years her husband's senior and still trying to hold on to something that could be no more. It was obvious that her husband was her world. He obviously loved her just as much, but he was already in communication with the woman who would probably become his next wife.

I don't believe there had been infidelity, but he was tired and ready for something new. There was a sound in his voice while on the phone with this woman that said that she would become more than just a friend when the time was right. Maybe the patient understood it as well, therefore, she rejected the thought of death and the possibility of being without him.

When I spoke to her privately, she did not identify herself as Catholic. She also was not ready to spiritually prepare for death via the last rites performed by a Catholic priest. She was also not receptive to chaplaincy. I initially thought she was also an atheist, but after spending time with her, I realized that she was also not an atheist. Her husband, Doug, was her god.

I spent at least a couple of hours at their home that afternoon. Family and neighbors were coming and going. Her husband was back with us at this point, and the other hospice staff were gone. I asked the patient to share how she and her husband had met to get a conversation going with her. Her husband, the self-proclaimed atheist, quickly took over the conversation.

He laughingly suggested that *someone up there,* motioning towards the ceiling, had to have orchestrated their meeting at a country club car show. It was obvious to me that he was trying his hardest to redirect the patient towards God, but she would not budge. She had no interest in exploring God-talk.

Her husband was a proud atheist, and they were seemingly bound together over atheism during their marriage. Her husband cultivated his unbelief with books, mentors, and other resources. The patient had seemingly never heard him make references to God in thirty years of marriage. Unlike him, she really didn't seem to have a clue that there is a God, nevertheless, a Savior of the world whom she could have a personal relationship with.

Her husband had been her god, and he knew it more than anyone. He had accepted and enjoyed the honor of such for the duration of their marriage, but as a previous Southern Baptist, he understood that she was in danger of Hell's fire, so he desperately tried to get someone else to help. This is why he requested the priest. After the patient rejected the priest, he wanted someone else to do something to save her, but she resisted.

The evening came, and I eventually ended my visit. The patient's husband walked me to the door. Since the patient had no interest in chaplaincy, I had no plans to return. I had no desire to force religion on her, but her husband was determined to get me a more private conversation with her. He thought that things would be different if I was alone with her. He asked me if I could return the following day, so I did.

When I returned, he went grocery shopping and left me home alone with the patient. She still had no interest in speaking with me about anything. She pretended to fall asleep. When her husband returned, I informed him that I would not return to see the patient. This was one of those times when I didn't discern Abba pressing the issue or tag-teaming me in specifically, and I wasn't sure why. On the other hand, Abba is a stickler for respecting freewill and this patient had already seemingly decided her fate and she was seemingly determined to stick with her decision.

I didn't schedule more visits, but I called and checked in with the patient's husband periodically. The last time I called, the patient wasn't doing well. I was in the area, so I drove by for a visit, more to support the patient's husband than to continue harassing the patient. The patient was still not receptive to chaplaincy, and I still didn't feel led by the Holy Spirit to press the issue with her. I had initially hoped that they both would turn to Jesus, but I did not witness that outcome for certain.

When I arrived, the patient's husband left me alone with her anyway, so I didn't waste any time. For her husband's sake, I kept trying. Again, I still didn't feel led by the Holy Spirit to press her. At this point, I was operating purely off the manipulations of the patient's husband and others. A member of our hospice team, who identified as Catholic, had also pressured me to pray an unsolicited salvation type of prayer over the patient and I had refused her.

Giving in to manipulation, I took a different approach with the patient this time and asked her directly if she believed that heaven was real. To my surprise, she said that she indeed did. I then asked her if it was somewhere that she wanted to go, but she didn't answer. After an uncomfortable pause, I asked her again.

She responded and said that she would need to think about whether heaven was somewhere she wanted to go or not. I was glad to hear it. It was the most relevant response that I had received from her. I reported the good news to her husband and agreed to return the following day. I told the patient that I would give her time to think about it, but it was too late.

She was actively dying when I returned, which means that she had been disconnected from the earthly realm in terms of her ability to communicate her thoughts effectively. Her eyes were glazed over. Her breathing was shallow. She was gasping for air, and she couldn't speak. She was still inside but primarily unable to engage my visit.

Her husband was still hopeful, so he left me alone with her again. I eventually prayed a salvation prayer over her without her consent since she could not verbally object to it. When I prayed over her, there was some reaction from her, a grunt of sorts, that led me to believe that she was not in agreement, but I'm not sure. Hopefully, she agreed because she transitioned while I was there.

I know my salvation prayer did not mean anything if she was not in agreement, but I prayed for her anyway. I wanted to go on record as doing such, just in case Jesus later had questions about it. I didn't want consequences for lack of action on my part. However, every sound-minded person can choose Christ or not. Holy Spirit doesn't force or pressure us, but He presents and records the opportunities presented.

In retrospect, I considered that when I asked her if she wanted to go to heaven, she didn't answer because she thought I was asking her if she was ready to die and go to heaven right then, and since she wasn't ready, she did not respond. This makes more sense to me and sounds better than the alternative, that she was playing mind games with me.

The patient surely heard and understood that I was colluding with her husband in efforts to trick her into a relationship with Jesus. She likely resented her husband for trying to resign from the position of being her god after thirty years of worship to him. When he tried to leave me alone with her, she spent the time calling his name, incessantly until he reappeared, which is why he opted to go to the grocery store during my visit. He was annoyed by her constant calling, but she refused to be comforted by anything aside from his presence. He was simply exhausted from being her personal god.

The hospice nurse was called back to the home to take care of her body and the business of her death. I stayed for the duration of such. I helped our nurse prepare her body for pickup. I wanted to help preserve what was important to her. I helped the nurse clean her up and we dressed her in her favorite color. The nurse did her makeup, as before, including putting on her favorite lipstick, and I placed her wig on her fuzzy head, just the way she would have wanted.

Another harsh reality about death is that the material things that we use to decorate our emptiness, look different on our lifeless bodies. She brought life and value to those things and value left when she breathed her last breath.

The mortuary arrived to pick her up, and she was gone. My sadness for her lingered. I stayed behind and talked with her husband. He walked me to the door and essentially blamed me for his wife not accepting Jesus as Savior. He stated that I didn't get back to her in time, while he had spent thirty years with her, pretending not to know that Jesus is God.

At the end of her life, I witnessed him trying, but she would not hear of it. I think he was just too ashamed to broach the subject with her directly or maybe he did, and she wasn't receptive. Of course, Holy Spirit undoubtedly sent many others throughout her lifetime or maybe Jesus Himself appealed to her. God is not above stooping down to get to us (Acts 9:1-5). This was a surprise to me. This was my first experience with this sort of thing; someone seemingly rejecting Christ at the very end when they had the opportunity to repent.

Romans 6:23 (ASV): For the wages of sin is death; but the free gift of God is eternal life in Christ Jesus our Lord.

I never would have thought that a dying person or a person in her situation would hesitate regarding the opportunity to accept Jesus Christ at the very end because that is what a lot of people hope for, a last-minute salvation plea. If given the option, most people *do not want* to spend their last days as a terminally ill hospice patient, but there is at least time for repentance or reconsideration in most of these cases.

On the other hand, most say that they prefer to die peacefully in their sleep or suddenly without a time of suffering, but that does not allow time for repentance. Therefore, these options need more thought. We can't have it both ways...just saying. We can never know for sure how or when death will come for us, so it would behoove us to plan in advance.

POW! (Pearls of Wisdom): Your words will testify for or against you on that day.

Chapter 6

Misguided Alliance

I entered the home of the new hospice patient, and I was left waiting at the front door for several minutes. I later learned that the hospice patient had not agreed to hospice chaplaincy. I figured out that her sons were forcing it on her. They were worried about her. She had been a pastor for over thirty years, but she refused visits from the ministers and members of her congregation. She was ashamed.

She believed and preached that divine health was a guaranteed benefit of her spirituality. She believed and preached that if sickness persisted, something was spiritually amiss with the afflicted one. Therefore, she could not face them after she was diagnosed with a terminal illness. It all came upon her suddenly. Understandably, her congregation was confused and bewildered. They wanted answers, and she didn't have any, so she refused their visits.

She was severely saddened and genuinely dumbfounded when the terminal illness came upon her. She had engaged her spirituality in ways that seemingly guaranteed healing and wellness. She would not talk to me extensively about her mixed beliefs, but she did share some spiritual encounters that she felt affirmed her beliefs.

She pastored a Christian church but mixed her Christianity with Buddhism and ancestral worship. Like many others, she never considered that the spirit beings that she communed with were demons disguised as spirit guides and ancestors, or maybe she did, but didn't care because she was temporarily getting her needs met. The devil is not faithful to his converts.

Isaiah 8:19 (WEB): When they tell you, "Consult with those who have familiar spirits and with the wizards, who chirp and who mutter," shouldn't a people consult with their God? Should they consult the dead on behalf of the living?

She believed that ancestors live perpetually in the spirit world, influencing the lives of descendants who give homage and call on them for help. She felt that her ancestors were a constant presence in her life, always communicating and directing her life steps. Much of her new approach to spirituality was picked up in seminary, in conjunction with her repeat international trips to West Africa to the church founded by the seminary she attended.

She had participated in a rebirth and/or a renaming ceremony and legally changed her name to solidify her newfound ancestral identity. She called out to her ancestors, but there was no apparent satisfactory answer after her terminal illness diagnosis. Her practice of ancestral worship failed her. She primarily died in isolation and shame. She was never able to face her congregation again.

When I started my hospice chaplain career, the Holy Spirit led me to settle some spiritual things if I was going to be able to work in the industry of slow death without bringing harm to my own spirituality. The Holy Spirit infused me with a knowing that God is good (Mark 10:19), and if God is good, everything He does is good, including allowing sickness and death, especially regarding long-term sickness and slow death.

In retrospect, it was like a light switch was turned on, and I don't know how or when, but one day, this suddenly became my reality. It became my unshakeable conviction in terms of sickness and death. I began to see long-term sickness and slow death as gifts from God. God's highest goal for humankind is that we are reconciled to Him through His Son, Jesus Christ, and everything God does or allows in this life works toward that end. Regardless of how bad or sorted the circumstances, I found that Holy Spirit is always at work making way for this higher purpose, especially in the most troubling of circumstances.

Romans 8:28 (ASV): And we know that to them that love God all things work together for good, even to them that are called according to his purpose.

Therefore, I approached every chaplain encounter with this in mind. I listen to see where the redemptive story is in play, and there are usually multiple. Jesus is always at work redeeming someone or something, a caregiver, a son, or a relationship. Every story has a redemptive aspect, and it's not always directly about the patient.

Exodus 34:14 (WEB): for you shall worship no other god; for Yahweh, whose name is Jealous, is a jealous God.

The patient's Muslim son began turning back towards Jesus during the patient's battle with terminal illness. Perhaps, the patient did as well, opting to get rid of her other gods. She had time to rethink her decisions and to abandon the other gods in her life, which is a requirement for inheriting eternal life. Even if she did not, Abba possibly mercifully allowed the sickness to be so that there was at least opportunity for her to do so. Holy Spirit pursues until the very end. Eternity lasts far longer than the years allotted to humankind on the earth. If Abba deems that a little or even a lot of suffering before death will help to bring us to reconciliation with Jesus, He is merciful enough to allow it. Many of my hospice patients were Christian Believers who had strayed, but were reconcile in sickness.

POW! (Pearls of Wisdom): God is not willing to be a part of a conglomerate of gods. He insists on being the only One on the throne in the hearts of His people.

49

Chapter 7

Bite of Death

The husband of the new hospice patient opened the front door and invited me inside. He announced who I was to the patient before whisking me around the corner to the eat-in kitchen. The living room had been transformed into the patient's bedroom. She was sitting up in bed watching television when I arrived.

There was a queen-sized canopy bed in the middle of the room. The bed had a white netted canopy on top. It was layered with white bed linen. The patient was dressed in a white babydoll-styled night gown. She closed the canopy, so I only got a glimpse of the patient, and she was beautiful.

She was a picture of beauty, class, and style. She was close to seventy, but she still had the face of a young girl. Once seated in the dining room, her husband disclosed to me that I would not be meeting her face-to-face.

She did not want anyone to see her in this less-than-perfect state. This was the life she had lived and the image that she wanted to maintain, even as a terminally ill hospice patient. Her medical team never figured out what was wrong with her, specifically. Her illness was a mystery. With the patient listening from the living room, I completed my spiritual assessment and ended my visit.

I was back within a week, providing grief support to the patient's husband. The patient died. They were not religious, so there was no religious community for him to lean on. I supposed that their lifestyle was their religion. A close friend, who was also an accountant, was there helping the patient's husband get his financial house back in order. The first thing on their list was to return the deceased patient's new Mercedes. The husband disclosed that the patient insisted on a new one every two years, and he was happy to give her what she wanted. He said that it was the price he had to pay to have someone of her caliber. He shared that her family was a part of New York's High Society. She was a distant heir to a cornflake dynasty.

The patient's husband was a commercial plumber. He disclosed that the company he worked for paid him good money but that his wife descended from royalty, so keeping her in the lifestyle that she was accustomed to was all that had mattered during the marriage. Their home was very modest, but it was in the same zip code as the rich and famous.

He paid for an image and an allusion of wealth including cosmetic surgeries, cars, clothes, jewelry, and country club memberships. The patient had spent her days at the country club perfecting her golf game, among other things. Her husband had to delay his grieving while his accountant worked to stop the hemorrhaging of his finances. *Bless his heart.*

Ecclesiastes 2:10-11 (WEB): Whatever my eyes desired, I didn't keep from them. I didn't withhold my heart from any joy, for my heart rejoiced because of all my labor, and this was my portion from all my labor. [11] Then I looked at all the works that my hands had worked, and at the labor that I had labored to do; and behold, all was vanity and a chasing after wind, and there was no profit under the sun.

I visited with him and provided grief support for a few months. His accountant was able to get things organized for him. By the time I ended my scheduled visits, he was ready to get back to the dating world. He was hoping to snag another strikingly beautiful White American woman. He even asked me if I knew someone.

The dental office that had installed the patient's six figure dental implants had settled the malpractice lawsuit that the patient's husband had brought against them. He suspected that the mystery terminal illness that had taken the patient's life had something to do with her new dental implants. The dental office apparently believed the same or at least didn't want the possibility of negative press regarding the issue. The patient's husband disclosed that her health failed, one thing at a time, after she had the implants installed. The implants cost the patient her life, but her looks remained until the end, as she would have wanted.

Matthew 16:26 (WEB): For what will it profit a man if he gains the whole world and forfeits his life? Or what will a man give in exchange for his life?

The interesting aspect of my meeting this patient and her husband was that I was in consultation for dental implants at the time I met them. I was obsessed with getting implants as well. I was willing to get all my teeth pulled out of my head so that I could replace them with implants because my crowns didn't match. I remember how desperate I felt at different times during this process.

I remember wondering if I could sell a kidney or something to get money for the implants. I inquired about grants and even sent the implantologist a personal letter recommending myself for free implants. Of course, he didn't agree to it. I also couldn't get buy-in from my husband. He was not receptive to me getting a mortgage-sized loan that would have been placed in my mouth as dental implants, but the Lord knew my resolve. I would have eventually figured something else out. *Bless my heart.*

1 John 2:16-17 (WEB): For all that is in the world—the lust of the flesh, the lust of the eyes, and the pride of life—isn't the Father's, but is the world's. [17] The world is passing away with its lusts, but he who does God's will remains forever.

I only realized the foolishness of what I called "faith" after I met this couple. I never asked the patient's husband the name of the office and the doctor who installed the patient's implants, but I was almost certain that it was the same office. They were a national leader in the industry at that time. The moral of the story is that our worldly obsessions can lead to premature death.

POW! (Pearls of Wisdom): Only Jesus can fill the holes in your soul. Nothing in this world can.

Chapter 8

Opt-Out

Flanked by an array of different flowers and various other plants and greenery, the front yard of the new hospice patient was impressive, to say the least. The couple had previously owned a flower shop, but they were forced to sell when the patient's health began to fail. Many of the replants in their yard had been left over from the sale of the business.

The patient was extremely emotional when I sat down with him to assess his spiritual needs. He wept for the entirety of my visit with him, but he refused to be comforted. The terminal illness diagnosis was devastating to him. It came out of nowhere, and it was very aggressive. There was not much time for processing. He learned of both the terminal illness and the death sentence at the same time. They had nothing to offer him in terms of a treatment plan. He was still in shock.

He identified as an atheist but disclosed that he was raised Baptist. He adopted atheism when he married his second wife. She was Hindu. Baptists are essentially monotheistic, worshipping one God. Hindus are polytheistic, worshipping many gods or deities, while atheists don't believe in God at all, but it was apparently what they agreed upon.

It was a mystery to me as to why he had to go as far as not believing in God at all. Surely, there was at least one deity he could have chosen from the Hindu faith. There are millions of them to choose from, but of course as a former Baptist he knew better than that. On the other hand, he wanted to appease her, so he opted completely out of religion, altogether. He refused to offend his wife by believing in Jesus. Understandably, this was likely the source of his angst. He no longer had a spiritual place to process during the most challenging time of his life.

Revelation 3:20 (WEB): Behold, I stand at the door and knock. If anyone hears my voice and opens the door, then I will come in to him and will dine with him, and he with me.

He shared that meeting his second wife was his greatest joy. They had a beautiful life together. His relationship with her was the reason for him sticking with his decision to forget Jesus, even in the face of death. With tears streaming down his face, he stated that turning back to Jesus would have been a betrayal to his wife of nine years and that he was not willing to do that to her.

I didn't ask him at that time, but in retrospect, I wonder how his alignment with Jesus would have hurt her. She was not walking around the house weeping uncontrollably as he was when I was there. She was very stoic and detached from his apparent pain. As a Hindu, there was no need for all that. Life would begin anew for *both* after his death.

He was committed to toughing it out, regardless of the consequences. I imagined that his attempt to forget the God who had walked with him throughout his lifetime, was equivalent to him trying to force an inflated beachball to stay underwater. It was apparent that he could not.

He was defiant in his declaration to remain an atheist, as if I was an enemy to his conviction. I wasn't. At this point in my chaplain career, I had encountered more than a few self-proclaimed atheists, and one thing they all had in common was that they were primarily well-versed or well-indoctrinated on the subject, so there was no compulsion for me to try to convert. They were more informed than me on the subject, so I had nothing but respect for the dedication. He understood what he wanted to believe, and I respected his bravery.

He was also a scientist, and I believe that no one knows better than the scientific community that God exists. It takes more faith to believe the Big Bang theory than it does to believe that God created the world with His words, in my opinion. Some believe the compromise that even if the Big Bang did happen, it was initiated by God. I was introduced to this theory or line of thinking in seminary, and I was somewhat intrigued by it, but it can't be true. It would make Genesis 1 a lie and I was delivered from unbelief after seminary. Therefore, God spoke the world into existence with His words, as recorded in the Bible. I now leave it at that.

This scientific community is trained to think a certain way, so there is a lot at stake if a member of this community decides to go off script and believe in the Bible and the God of the Bible. They could lose a lot, including career, the respect of peers, community, and apparently spouse, among other things. Therefore, ignorance is a choice in many cases, especially this one.

I don't believe it's possible to unknow Jesus. This patient had been made spiritually alive at an earlier time in his life. I felt a spiritual connection to him. He was not spiritually unaware although he wanted to be, which is why he was so distressed, at this point.

There is no struggle with those who genuinely don't believe God exists. They walk towards death believing that the lights will go out and that they will go forever into unconsciousness and nothingness, never to live again. This was not the case with this patient. He was fighting to *not* know and seemingly seeking a fight with me about his atheism and it was not my first time encountering someone like him. It was becoming commonplace for me in the context of chaplaincy.

I have encountered more than one atheists who was disturbed by my unwillingness to fight with them in terms of trying to win them to faith in Jesus. I am a supporter of religious choice because I don't like anyone telling me what I should believe. It can be disrespectful.

The times that I encountered this situation, the atheists noted that their friends and families were always trying to convince them to try Jesus, and they seemed to have enjoyed the pursuit, but I had no pursuit in these cases. It was as if they wanted me to be offended that they rejected the God I served as an ambassador for, but I was not. Their unbelief was not my business. It is the Holy Spirit's job to convict of sin. Jesus gives us freewill in hopes that we will choose Him, but the choice is left to each individual.

John 16:7-9 (WEB): Nevertheless I tell you the truth: It is to your advantage that I go away; for if I don't go away, the Counselor won't come to you. But if I go, I will send him to you. ⁸ When he has come, he will convict the world about sin, about righteousness, and about judgment; ⁹ about sin, because they don't believe in me

Jesus doesn't have low self-esteem. He is the prize. His "Godness" is not contingent upon the beliefs and opinions of humankind and nor is He diminished because of the unbelief of atheists. He still loves them, but I advise against verbalizing such. It is rude to tell someone who doesn't believe in God that you will pray to God for them. There is no need to verbalize such. I learned the hard way.

Jesus is not running around begging and pleading with us to love Him back. Observe how he moved about in the Gospels. He was not forceful in His presentation. He demonstrated His "Godness" and left the decision to follow Him to each individual. Furthermore, it was documented early in time (Genesis 6), that humanity's bend towards evil was even grievous to God. Therefore, He knows full well what He is dealing with, which is why Jesus came.

1 John 2:2 (ASV): and he is the propitiation for our sins; and not for ours only, but also for the whole world.

He is desperate for us, but not dependent on us. His "Godness" is not shattered by our lack of response to Him. Knowing and loving God through Jesus is a benefit to us. He is the self-existing One. Haven't you heard! In Psalm 50:12, God reminds us that if He was hungry, He wouldn't come to us because He owns everything. In Luke 19:40, Jesus told the people that if the people didn't praise Him, the rocks would. Therefore, at this point, my exchange with this type was almost comical. They wanted a fight, and I had none for them.

I was providing spiritual support to a dementia hospice patient who was in an assisted living facility. Her dementia was advancing to a point where I was losing meaningful connection with her. She was a strong Christian Believer, but I needed new ways to connect with her as her dementia progressed. Therefore, I called her husband for insight on how to continue engaging her spirituality. I inquired about her spiritual disciplines, the music she liked, hobbies, etc.

When I called her husband, I introduced myself as the hospice chaplain who had been providing spiritual care to his wife at the facility. He stated that someone had apparently made a mistake because they should have informed me that he was an atheist. I expressed to him that I saw that information in the notes, but that I wasn't calling to discuss that, but to discuss his wife. I stated that I was calling him in hopes of learning new ways of spiritually connecting with his wife.

He responded by telling me that he didn't go to church, but that he watched Dr. Charles Stanley on television. He also disclosed that his housekeeper continuously ministered to him, and he went on and on trying to lure me into a conversation about his spirituality, but I would not go there with him, but he persisted. I eventually said to him: *"Sir, I saw in the notes that you are an atheist. I also saw that you identify as a "cross-dresser" who prefers male pronouns, but I didn't call about that. I don't care about all of that, anyway. I called you to learn more about your wife, God's daughter, my sister. Since you're busy, God sent others to walk with her on this end-of-life journey while you sit home eating bon-bons and playing dress up, so if you don't mind, can we get back to the business of your wife.*

I didn't say any of that, but I wanted to. Instead, I spent at least an hour on the phone with him listening to him try to navigate his guilt for walking contrary to what he knew to be truth. I tried to wrangle information about his wife out of him, but to no avail. When I asked him something about the patient, he responded with something about himself, and this went on for a while.

I don't recall getting any relevant information from him about his wife. He couldn't move past information about himself. He expected me to join him in trying to talk himself out of his decision to reject Jesus, but the Holy Spirit didn't lead me to do so. He wasn't my fish. Again, every atheist that I have encountered in the context of chaplaincy has been resolute regarding what and why they believe what they believe, and I had no compulsion to fight with them about it. The things of God are spiritually understood.

1 Corinthians 1:18 (WEB): For the word of the cross is foolishness to those who are dying, but to us who are being saved it is the power of God.

I noticed another commonality in these instances The atheists often had a Christian background, and they felt some disappointment towards Jesus because of the suffering that had been inflicted on someone they loved. Someone whom they loved, had loved Jesus and He had allowed some heinous situation to overtake the person or persons. In essence, they were angry at God on behalf of others, and I was ok with that too. Jesus is able to fight His own battles.

Furthermore, I was also initially surprised at the number of times one of the partners in a marital relationship chose their spouse over a relationship or intimacy with Holy Spirit. Of course, they wouldn't call it that. These decisions are usually indirect patterns of action over time. The person can and does fool himself or herself into believing that it is not what it is, but it was not indirect with this patient. It was direct. His decision gave real-life meaning to being consciously willing to go to Hell for someone.

Matthew 10:32-33 (ASV): Every one therefore who shall confess me before men, him will I also confess before my Father who is in heaven. [33] But whosoever shall deny me before men, him will I also deny before my Father who is in heaven.

He died days after my visit with him. I often wonder if he reconciled with Jesus and hid it from his wife, but I don't think that works. True Believers are usually not trying to hide such great news. The redeemed of the Lord, want to say so (Psalm 107:2)!

POW! (Pearls of Wisdom): Jesus is desperate for us, so much so, that He died on a cross to save us, but He will not override freewill.

Section Three
Interrupted by
Love

Chapter 9

The Sons and Daughters of Abraham

The hospital room in the Intensive Care Unit was packed full of a team of medical professionals who were in discussions regarding extreme life-saving measures for the mother of six. They were considering transforming her room in the Intensive Care Unit into an Operating Room because they couldn't risk moving her. She was too sick. I was on-call and working the overnight shift as a hospital chaplain intern when I received a referral to visit with this family.

The staff wanted a chaplain to provide spiritual support to the patient's husband when he returned. When he left the hospital the night before, his wife was doing well and on schedule to be discharged. She was now septic. When he returned to the hospital, he was told to prepare for the worst.

I sat with him as he made calls to family members. He identified as Muslim and remained very stoic as he contacted family and friends to share the sad news. The lounge designated for the family and friends of ICU patients was eventually filled with family and friends from the Muslim community. They mourned and performed the appropriate rituals necessitated in times of looming death. The show of support was moving.

Alternating between family in the patient's room and those in the waiting lounge, I ran into the doctor who had charge over the patient's care before she was transferred to the ICU. We met initially in the unit where the woman was prior to this medical emergency. We greeted each other and discovered that we were both in the ICU to see the same family. He disclosed that he was on his way off duty, where he would be for the next seven days. He had delayed the start of his vacation because he wanted to check on this patient. The ICU doctor had taken charge of the patient's care, but this unit doctor wanted to see and meet with the family. He was also Muslim. Together, we went to visit the family in the waiting lounge.

When we entered the waiting lounge, the adult male friends and family members of the patient gathered around the doctor and listened to him with trust and familiarity that was palpable. He updated them on the patient's condition, expressing that it was equivalent to someone running full speed towards a cliff but that the medical team was doing everything possible to save her.

They received his words as if they were honey dripping from a honeycomb, even asking him if he could be the patient's doctor, instead of the ICU doctor. He explained that he would want the same doctor they had if it was his family member in crisis. The doctor spoke with such care and compassion that my eyes watered.

Psalm 8:4 (WEB): what is man, that you think of him? What is the son of man, that you care for him?

His humility moved me because he had not been on the scene to witness the callousness of the ICU doctor. He seemed to have lacked empathy and compassion, but he was a phenomenal physician, according to all. He was recognized for saving lives and was the best of the best, they said, but he unapologetically took no time for the messiness of human pain and emotion. He left such care to the others.

The husband of the dying woman was in shock. The night before, he had kissed his beautiful, healthy wife and mother of his six children good night, only to return and learn that she was in septic shock and probably not going to survive it. When he asked the ICU doctor to speak on the phone with his wife's sister, who was calling from outside the country, with indignation in his voice, the doctor asked if she was a doctor. Learning that she was not, the doctor turned and walked away without saying another word. A few minutes later, another doctor approached. The doctor sent her back to attend to such matters.

The doctor visiting from the other unit knew nothing of what transpired before his arrival, but Holy Spirit did and sent this Muslim doctor to comfort this Muslim family. The unit doctor was obviously familiar with the strong communal aspects of the Muslim community. He was a part of that community and was sent by Jesus Himself to comfort them in their time of bewilderment.

This was my first time seeing Jesus in this way. This was not the Jesus I learned about in church. Church Jesus had a chip on his shoulder. This Jesus used a Muslim doctor to attend to the needs of a Muslim family but on Jesus' behalf. I discovered at this moment that Jesus is busy out in the world indiscriminately loving and attending to all kinds of people regardless of nationality, race, gender, and even religious affiliation. He also doesn't care if people acknowledge Him for it or not. He does it anyway because that is what love does.

I realized that Jesus wanted me to see Him in this light because it informed my chaplain ministry. This encounter took place early in my chaplain career, during my first chaplain assignment. It exposed me to how Jesus works in the world, and it freed me to do the same; provide spiritual care without prejudice. I didn't know that Jesus loves people of other religions the way that He does. Of course, no one told me this. I just never saw it up close in this way.

I unknowingly thought that Christians owned the patent on Jesus' love, but it's not true. Jesus loves everyone and often uses all kinds of other human beings to affirm this love. I have seriously considered, over the years, if the ICU doctor called the Muslim doctor to the case because of the Muslim doctor's connection to the Muslim community. The ICU doctor was Jewish and likely even more familiar than most with the strength of community. In either case, Jesus gets to hurting people who need Him by any means necessary. He strategically places people, Christian and non-Christian, all over the globe to aid Him in bringing comfort to humankind because that's what love does.

My shift ended, so the next on-call chaplain continued to provide spiritual care to this family. The patient died, so the other chaplain was there in the waiting lounge with the family and faith community for several hours. She had a different experience with the patient's husband.

When I initially met with the patient's husband, we were alone in a small private room in the ICU reserved for the close family members of patients who were in crisis. I sat with him as he made phone calls to family members. He was distraught, so every now and again, he forgot the Islamic religious and gender barriers that were supposed to be between us. He would randomly reach out and touch my hand, leg, or arm. He did it a few times, but he would snatch his hand back when he remembered that there were rules against such.

Isaiah 66:13a (WEB): As one whom his mother comforts, so I will comfort you.

His religion had not prepared him for the excruciating pain of suddenly losing his wife and the mother of his children. He was visibly shaken and in need of comfort, but he did not allow himself to collapse at this time. By the time the other chaplain got to him, his wife was dead, so he threw all of that out the window. I was told that he touched, hugged, and cried in her arms like a baby as he tried to grapple with his new reality. His religion didn't stand a chance. He laid aside Islam and received the love and support that Jesus sent him, via a team of others with different religious beliefs than him, the other natural and spiritual children of Abraham.

POW! (Pearls of Wisdom): Christians do not own the patent on Jesus' love. Jesus does and He shares it with everyone, indiscriminately and without reservation.

Chapter 10

The Doctor

I was on-call and working the overnight shift as a hospital chaplain at the hospital when I came across a referral to see a terminally ill patient who had been admitted to the hospital. It was almost midnight, but I took a chance and went to see the patient in hopes that he would still be awake, and he was.

He was awake and very much in control of his care. By profession, he was a physician in a different hospital system. When I arrived for my visit, he was directing his nurse to do this or that thing. He disclosed that he had received a death sentence with only two weeks to live. He wanted continued spiritual support, so I returned the following day.

He was sitting in bed when I arrived. I continued cultivating a relationship with him and facilitated storytelling. He first identified himself as a homosexual man; likely to see my reaction as a religious representative. He was in a thirty-year union with another homosexual man. He shared that he had abandoned his Catholic faith because it didn't fit his new lifestyle. He shared that he didn't necessarily want to legalize his same-sex marriage but acquiesced after the terminal illness prognosis to appease his partner.

He disclosed that he was surprised by the terminal illness because he had been careful to take care of himself. He disclosed that as a homosexual man, statistically, he was more at risk for certain diseases and viruses. Therefore, to minimize the risk of such, he lived a clean lifestyle, eating a healthy diet, exercising regularly, practicing sexual monogamy, and attending regular doctor visits, etc. He had done everything he knew to do, but his efforts were not a match for the terminal illness.

I am not sure what triggered him, but out of nowhere, he went on an unprovoked rant about his perceived failures of the Black American community, specifically what he considered "low-performing" Black American males. He considered Black American men lazy and perpetually in wait of their baby momma's welfare check due on the first of every month. He said some other cruel things, which I honestly can't recall. He suddenly stopped the rant and moved on to another subject as suddenly as he had started.

Like you are right now, I thought I was in the *Twilight Zone*. I considered that he had slipped out of his mind, which was not unusual for someone at end-of-life, but he wasn't close enough to death for that. He was still walking around giving orders to the nursing staff.

He was obviously frustrated that he had not beaten the illness in his second round with it. He took the liberty of trying to punch it out with me instead. He offended me intentionally, but before I could respond, Jesus interrupted my thoughts with a question, "Are you going to choose to be offended, or are you going to do what I sent you there to do?"

I was too offended to ask Jesus what He sent me there to do. I did not have the wherewithal to care. Hell seemed like the right place for the doctor under the circumstances. I spent at least 45 minutes listening to him talk, while I meditated on the offense. I brought the visit to a close by asking him if there was anything I could do for him. Of course, I had no desire to do anything for him. I was only signaling to him that I was ending the visit.

He responded by asking me if I would pray for him. It's not unusual for sick and dying people to do that, so with a hint of apathy in my tone, I asked him what it was exactly that he wanted God to do for him. He asked me to pray that he wouldn't be afraid when the time came for him to die, and my heart broke into pieces. I wasn't expecting that.

I understood at that moment that Abba was teaching me something. Among other things, he was teaching me that just as the Holy Spirit had boots strapped on and was walking up and down the halls and in and out of the hospital rooms attending to the needs of people without discrimination, the devil was moving about doing the same.

Jesus shows up strong in these life-and-death situations, but so does the enemy, specifically when his converts are involved. The devil fights for ownership of the souls that have demonstrated allegiance to him, especially as the curtain closes on life in the natural realm. The Holy Spirit is God, so He can be anywhere He wants to be, and since He is omnipresent, He actually can't not be somewhere. Jesus was obviously on the scene, still reaching out to the doctor, hoping to interrupt the last act of his life.

Ephesians 6:12 (ASV): For our wrestling is not against flesh and blood, but against the principalities, against the powers, against the world-rulers of this darkness, against the spiritual hosts of wickedness in the heavenly places.

The devil was there with the doctor when I got there, propping him up with pride. For at least 40 of the 45 minutes that I spent with him, he went on and on about his accomplishments as a man, doctor, serviceman, and activist. He was very proud of himself. He disclosed that at some point in his life, he thought he was God, the master of his own destiny, but at this point in his life, he realized that he had been deceived.

Proverbs 17:28 (WEB): Even a fool, when he keeps silent, is counted wise. When he shuts his lips, he is thought to be discerning.

Jesus held my mouth shut to the point that the doctor likely saw my silence as strength opposed to what was really going on in my mind and heart. My silence was not my wisdom. I was meditating on the offense.

Romans 10:11-13 (ASV): For the scripture saith, Whosoever believeth on him shall not be put to shame. [12] For there is no distinction between Jew and Greek: for the same Lord is Lord of all, and is rich unto all that call upon him: [13] for, Whosoever shall call upon the name of the Lord shall be saved.

My failure to react made him feel safe with me, safe and vulnerable enough to disclose his fear and to ask me to ask Jesus to help him. His sexuality had driven every major decision in his adult life, including him abandoning his Catholic faith. On this day, he laid down his sexuality and asked Jesus for help.

POW! (Pearls of Wisdom): The devil does not stand down when you or your loved-one is seeking to be reconciled with Jesus. He ramps up his efforts, but so must you, but in the authority of Jesus' name.

Chapter 11

The Engineer

The hospice patient opened his front door and invited me inside. He had been adamant in his communications with the hospice medical director regarding not wanting chaplain visits, not even the assessment. Chaplain visits weren't mandatory, but the assessment was, so he allowed the one visit.

I facilitated storytelling and provided active listening as we sat in his living room drinking iced tea. He was an atheist and for that reason he rejected spiritual support. He disclosed that he didn't believe in prayer. He felt that prayer gave false hope and manipulated emotions, so he had no need for it. He was an engineer, so he preferred real-world solutions. He also did his research and opted to reject the medications used in hospice care to bring patients comfort as the pain of terminal illness increased.

We sat and talked about random things. It was an election year, so that's what we talked about primarily. Like the doctor before him, he suddenly went off on a rant, also attacking the Black American community, but I was more prepared for it this time.

Proverbs 29:11 (WEB): A fool vents all of his anger, but a wise man brings himself under control.

This encounter took place two years after my encounter with the doctor. I was more familiar with the schemes of the devil at this time. I also better understood the tag-team relationship that the Holy Spirit allowed me to be a part of with Him, so I was not offended or altogether surprised this time.

The patient did not believe in God. He was not a Christian Believer. He had not surrendered his life to Jesus, so his soul had been released to the evil one. His soul belonged to another. By default, saying "no" to Jesus is saying "yes" to the god of this world, Satan, also known as the devil (Ephesians 2:1-2). We should not be surprised when the demonic possessor of a soul speaks out and fights for continued occupancy. This ugly behavior is not exclusively your teenager, your spouse, or your manager. These people don't know that their souls have been hijacked and invaded by the devil. I know it's hard to hear, but these are facts. I don't want you to be deceived. We are all created by God, but we are not all children of God, unless we choose to be.

John 1:12 (WEB): But as many as received him, to them he gave the right to become God's children, to those who believe in his name:

I discovered that the patient's wife had died months earlier, and she also had a terminal illness. Someone had likely prayed for her, but she still died, so the devil exploited his pain. This was obviously a sore spot for him. His hurt was deeper than what was on the surface. The adversarial spirit in him was willing to launch an attack against me, as God's representative, while I had nothing to do with his situation.

James 4:7 (WEB): Be subject therefore to God. Resist the devil, and he will flee from you.

Therefore, I was not impacted by his statements. I don't remember what he said, but I wasn't flooded by negative emotions as I had been before. Unfortunately, the devil knew that rejection was something that I struggled with, so it was what he used to disarm me, but it didn't work this time. The devil, the accuser of the brethren (Revelation 12:10) is also aware of your soul struggles, so he will try and disarm you with such when you are in battle for the souls of others. Fortunately, I understood that I was on assignment. Like the doctor before him, the patient stopped his rant as suddenly as he had begun. He resumed civilized conversation as if the diatribe had not occurred, and so did I.

By the end of our visit, the patient who disclosed to me that he didn't believe in God or prayer asked me to pray for him, so I did. He was able to lay down his unbelief and agree with Jesus' chosen way of intervention in his situation, prayer. He lived another year and rode his bike daily up until two weeks before he died. He was granted another year to consider a relationship with Jesus.

POW! (Pearls of Wisdom): Resistance is a weapon of warfare against the devil.

Chapter 12

The Congressman

I entered the room of a patient who was in the hospital for observation. He had some sort of episode, so his doctor ordered more tests to assess his situation further. It was early in the morning when I dropped by to conduct a spiritual assessment. The patient was awake, so I proceeded with the assessment.

He was receptive to a conversation about spirituality. I was a chaplain intern in the hospital setting, so I diligently followed my spiritual assessment tool of choice, FICA. I asked about his faith, its importance to him, faith community involvement, and an action plan for us to address his spiritual needs.

His faith was important to him, but it didn't require a specific place of worship. It was very individualized. I can't recall how he classified his spiritually, but it had something to do with the energy being transmitted from rays of sunlight, I think. I was curious about other faiths, so I allowed him to explain it to me. I was still in seminary at this time. I understood that no one person knows everything there is to know about everything, so I was teachable. I was still curious about the spiritual constructs of others, at the time.

Later in my professional chaplain career I encountered a professional atheist chaplain. I met him at a chaplain conference. He was indorsed by The Humanist Society. He was a guest speaker at the conference. I was intrigued by the idea of an atheist chaplain, so I sat on the front row and gave my full attention. I was so attentive that when I spoke to him one-on-one afterwards, he thought I was a possible convert. I assured him that I was all about believing in Jesus.

From what I could ascertain from his presentation, it was likely his grandmother's seeming fanatical church-life approach to religion that turned him off, but those same fanatical church disciplines were still sustaining him. He was board certified and seemed to be an exceptional chaplain. His grandmother raised him to know Jesus. He was as serious about his commitment to provide unbiased spiritual care and his call to professional chaplaincy as I was. Honoring the story of others over your own is true spiritual care, which is what I offered the Congressman.

Revelation 5:8 (WEB Now when he had taken the book, the four living creatures and the twenty-four elders fell down before the Lamb, each one having a harp, and golden bowls full of incense, which are the prayers of the saints.

I spent at least thirty-five minutes listening to him and asking questions about his interesting approach to spirituality. It was too far out there for me to understand, so I mostly listened. As a professional chaplain, my role is to support spiritual care seekers in their preferred faith traditions or religions. Explaining his faith to me gave him immense joy. I never dismiss anyone's faith journey. I seek connection and understanding, instead.

A veteran once shared with me his near-death-experience. He authored a book about it. During his experience, he was transported to both Heaven and then Hell or vice versa. He assured me that aliens are real and that they have an abode in the heavenlies. He saw them on his way up to the third Heaven, where he met with and had a conversation with Father God Himself. He reported that Father God doesn't have a physical body but that His presence permeates Heaven.

He also shared that he saw the devil when he was transported to Hell. He reported that the devil is housed in a body of sorts and that the devil identified himself as homosexual. He shared that the devil had a make-out session with a same sex creature whom the devil referred to as his wife. I would never dismiss a patient's literal or figurative dreams or experiences. Like Mary, I ponder such things. On the other hand, I press in for clarity when it is a professing Christian, but not in an offensive way.

1 Corinthians 5:9-13 (WEB): I wrote to you in my letter to have no company with sexual sinners; [10] yet not at all meaning with the sexual sinners of this world, or with the covetous and extortionists, or with idolaters, for then you would have to leave the world. [11] But as it is, I wrote to you not to associate with anyone who is called a brother who is a sexual sinner, or covetous, or an idolater, or a slanderer, or a drunkard, or an extortionist. Don't even eat with such a person. [12] For what do I have to do with also judging those who are outside? Don't you judge those who are within? [13] But those who are outside, God judges. "Put away the wicked man from among yourselves."

There was a more senior chaplain working within the same Clinical Pastoral Education program as me during this internship. She identified as homosexual, and she and her wife were senior pastors of a local Christian church. I was still in seminary at this time, so the idea of homosexual Christian pastors was still an anomaly to me.

I had a cordial relationship with this woman, probably more *cordial* than I knew. Prior to my knowledge that she identified as homosexual, I cultivated a somewhat casual sisterly work relationship with her. I openly and innocently initiated and enjoyed sisterly hugs from her, when I saw her at work. She was known more for her radical Christian conversion story. She transitioned from a career as a celebrated neuroscientist to professional Christian ministry.

I don't recall how, but I discovered that she identified as homosexual. She didn't try to hide it. I just didn't know. We were in different chaplain cohorts. When I confirmed it with my cohort supervisor, she disclosed that she figured that I didn't know. Fortunately, or unfortunately I was not able to conceal my identity as a Christian who believed the Bible although I was vigilant regarding my intentionality of not offending others who held alternate beliefs.

To do so, would have been the premature death of my professional chaplain career. The professional chaplain program was essentially designed to weed out those who couldn't see past their own beliefs and that was no longer me. My supervisor assumed that I would not have cultivated a relationship with a woman who identified as homosexual, but she was only partly correct. Christians are warned to disassociate with Christians who persist in such.

1 Corinthians 5:9-13 (WEB): I wrote to you in my letter to have no company with sexual sinners; [10] yet not at all meaning with the sexual sinners of this world, or with the covetous and extortionists, or with idolaters, for then you would have to leave the world. [11] But as it is, I wrote to you not to associate with anyone who is called a brother who is a sexual sinner, or covetous, or an idolater, or a slanderer, or a drunkard, or an extortionist. Don't even eat with such a person. [12] For what do I have to do with also judging those who are outside? Don't you judge those who are within? [13] But those who are outside, God judges. "Put away the wicked man from among yourselves."

However, at this point, I saw my relationship with the woman as an opportunity for understanding, so I took advantage of it. She was a reasonable, intelligent, and mature woman. I had enough of a relationship with her that she would not have taken offense to my questions about her sexual preference. I desired enlightenment, as well. I considered that she had received additional insight from Jesus, the God of the Bible regarding the permissibility of her transgressing His command to not practice homosexuality, so I invited her to dinner and asked her such.

She justified her homosexual lifestyle and viewed her sin as being exonerated by the death and resurrection of Jesus, which covers all sin, past, present, and future. She proposed that sin is no longer an issue for any professing Christian from God's perspective. Professing Christians are free to continue sinning because Jesus already paid for all sin, she believed.

1 Corinthians 6:9-11 (WEB): Or don't you know that the unrighteous will not inherit God's Kingdom? Don't be deceived. Neither the sexually immoral, nor idolaters, nor adulterers, nor male prostitutes, nor homosexuals, [10] nor thieves, nor covetous, nor drunkards, nor slanderers, nor extortionists, will inherit God's Kingdom. [11] Some of you were such, but you were washed. You were sanctified. You were justified in the name of the Lord Jesus, and in the Spirit of our God.

I didn't go into such details with her, but aside from God's command against it, I don't have any especially deep or intellectual objections to argue against the sexual practice of homosexuality. It really doesn't matter anyway. Creator God's command is the only relevant objection that matters in this discussion anyway.

It seems to be commonsense to me considering how God designed the male and female bodies. The practicing of such just doesn't make sense to me anatomically. The male-to-male and female-to-female sexual activity is not congruent with the physicality of the male and female anatomy. Surprised at her response, I proposed to her that if homosexuality isn't a sin, then sin doesn't exist.

Leviticus 18:22 (WEB): "'You shall not lie with a man as with a woman. That is detestable.

Her response to that was simple. Exactly, sin doesn't exist, she said. I really couldn't believe what I was hearing. Not only does sin not exists, but she also disclosed that she did not use the Bible as her primary source of spiritual enlightenment at her church. She selected favorable texts from it, and ignored the rest, supplementing her teachings with extrabiblical texts, instead. This is crazy, I thought, but I managed to continue dialogue with her, eventually moving on to other things.

I have had several friends in my life who practiced homosexuality. The interesting thing is that the one who didn't profess Jesus as Lord is the only one who considered the practicing of homosexuality sin. He had not forsaken his Christian upbringing and commonsense in that regard. He understood it for what it was.

On the other hand, many professing homosexual Christians try to socialize the Gospel of Jesus Christ and try to bully and to persecute the rest of us when we don't agree. They are committed to changing God's word to fit the lifestyle which in essence is demonic. I believe it would be better if they started their own religion like Joseph Smith, who founded Mormonism, Charles Taze Russell, who founded Jehovah Witnesses, Siddhartha Gautama, who founded Buddhism, or Muhammad, who founded Islam, instead of trying to hijack and corrupt Christianity.

We had this discussion over a meal outside of work, but I must admit that she presented differently away from the hospital. She was more spiritually exposed. Either she manifested or my eyes were opened to the spiritual implications of her lifestyle. It was a cordial exchange, but the perversion was more pronounced. She was intentional in the way she handled her fork with her tongue after finishing her dessert. Her last move with her eating utensil gave me clarity regarding who she was. She was deceived, but also a willing participant in also deceiving others and actively looking for others to devour.

1 John 3:3-10 (WEB): Everyone who has this hope set on him purifies himself, even as he is pure. ⁴ Everyone who sins also commits lawlessness. Sin is lawlessness. ⁵ You know that he was revealed to take away our sins, and no sin is in him. ⁶ Whoever remains in him doesn't sin. Whoever sins hasn't seen him and doesn't know him. [7] Little children, let no one lead you astray. He who does righteousness is righteous, even as he is righteous. [8] He who sins is of the devil, for the devil has been sinning from the beginning. To this end the Son of God was revealed: that he might destroy the works of the devil. [9] Whoever is born of God doesn't commit sin, because his seed remains in him, and he can't sin, because he is born of God. [10] In this the children of God are revealed, and the children of the devil. Whoever doesn't do righteousness is not of God, neither is he who doesn't love his brother.

I was literally sickened with the urge to vomit at the table when I caught sight of whatever that was that she was doing with her tongue and fork. I had to remove myself from the table to hurry outside where I dry-heaved like a dog for several minutes. This was the Holy Spirit's way of revealing to me the diabolical nature of this sisterly woman. I didn't need to ponder this situation. I understood where she stood. I considered the innocent new Christians at her church who were searching for clarity and truth.

Matthew 18:4-6 (WEB): Whoever therefore humbles himself as this little child is the greatest in the Kingdom of Heaven. [5] Whoever receives one such little child in my name receives me, [6] but whoever causes one of these little ones who believe in me to stumble, it would be better for him if a huge millstone were hung around his neck and that he were sunk in the depths of the sea.

Fortunately, the Congressman was not seeking to deceive, so my conversation with him ended differently. My conversation with him was eventually interrupted by a phone call that he had to answer and attend to. Before leaving him to his phone call, I asked him if I could pray for him, but that I wanted to pray to "my" God, Jesus.

As a chaplain, I generally don't offer prayer to spiritual care seekers, unless they ask. It is rude to offer prayer to someone who doesn't believe in God, but it was another prompting of the Holy Spirit. He was not offended. The Congressman jovially waved his hand towards me and said, "Sure, whatever you want!"

Proverbs 11:30b (WEB): He who is wise wins souls.

Abba was teaching me something at this moment. Kindness shown to another person is the introduction to our Jesus. Listening gets us inside the door of their hearts. The patient was open to my God because I listened to him. I didn't agree or disagree; I just listened to him. As a result, he was able to receive my prayer to my God on his behalf, the God that he didn't particularly believe existed.

POW! (Pearls of Wisdom): Your kindness is the introduction to your God.

Section Four
The Cost

Chapter 13

Wicked Witnesses

I walked down the stairs into the beautifully remolded living space of the new hospice patient. Her daughter and son-in-law upgraded the space to accommodate the patient's changing needs. The patient's terminal illness was progressing slowly, but they felt it was time to call in hospice care. I conducted the spiritual assessment with the patient and her adult daughter. They were both Jehovah's Witnesses, but they opted for additional chaplain visits, understanding that I had a different faith than theirs.

The patient had the hospice diagnosis, so she was more introspective about her beliefs. Regardless of religion, a person facing death is prone to examine and reexamine what their religion has to say about death or what happens afterwards. Being present with the Lord after the death of the body (2 Corinthians 5:8), according to the Bible and the Christian faith, versus ceasing to exist, according to Jehovah's Witnesses dogma, is something to think about.

As the weeks and months passed, they seemed to be the ones being converted. Of course no one would ever say such. The patient's son-in-law likely suspected such, so he sat in on some of my visits. He was the lifelong Witness who brought these two into the religion. He was well established in the religion generationally, so defecting was not an option for any of them. They were bonded to the community, but Jesus can replace community.

Matthew 19:29 (WEB): Everyone who has left houses, or brothers, or sisters, or father, or mother, or wife, or children, or lands, for my name's sake, will receive one hundred times, and will inherit eternal life.

In the hospital setting, I have had the pleasure of serving some wonderful faith-filled Christian Believers hiding out among and disguised as Jehovah's Witnesses. They never hesitated to yield to the voice of Jesus regarding receiving lifesaving blood transfusions for themselves and their family members, which is traditionally forbidden by the religion. Of course, it wasn't information that they testified about at Kingdom Hall.

The close communal ties seem to be the most significant aspect of the religion, which successfully cultivates a sense of belonging. Jehovah's Witnesses do life together but, they run the risk of being officially excommunicated from the community if they stray from the paths that have been designated for the religion. A lifetime of relationships is gone in that instant, for those who transgress these rules. Therefore, defectors continue the charade for the sake of keeping community, to their own detriment, and unfortunately, for the sake of a lie.

John 10:30 (WEB): I and the Father are one."

A central claim for the religion is that Jesus was an exceptional human being, but He is not God while the Scriptures demonstrates otherwise. The religion deceitfully presents this difference as miniscule and the spiritually ignorant signs on, but it is wickedly devastating to the Christian faith. The religion's strategy for debunking the truth of Jesus being God incarnate is to suggests that Jesus doesn't explicitly claim to be God, while He demonstrates it.

Mark 14:61-63 (WEB): But he stayed quiet, and answered nothing. Again the high priest asked him, "Are you the Christ, the Son of the Blessed?" ⁶² Jesus said, "I am. You will see the Son of Man sitting at the right hand of Power, and coming with the clouds of the sky." ⁶³ The high priest tore his clothes and said, "What further need have we of witnesses? (Also, Matthew 26:63-65, Luke 22:67-71, John 10:30-38)

The high priest indignantly tore his robe because he knew the Hebrew Scriptures. Jesus answers affirmatively and then apply to Himself messianic prophesies from the Hebrew Scriptures/Old Testament. Jesus used the title "I AM", the same name that the God of Abraham, Isaac, and Jacob used to identify Himself when Moses asked Him His name.

Exodus 3:13-14 (WEB): Moses said to God, "Behold, when I come to the children of Israel, and tell them, 'The God of your fathers has sent me to you,' and they ask me, 'What is his name?' what should I tell them?" [14] God said to Moses, "I AM WHO I AM," and he said, "You shall tell the children of Israel this: 'I AM has sent me to you.'"

Jesus attributes to Himself the language of both Psalm 110:1 and Daniel 7:13-14, passages that prophesy of the Messiah being human yet divine. Also, coming with the clouds is a symbol of divine authority and the Son of man is given glory, a kingdom, and dominion over the whole world, which is parallel to God's kingdom. Surely, Jesus understood the impact of His statement. He was submitting to His appointment with His death, burial, and resurrection.

Psalm 110:1 (WEB): Yahweh says to my Lord, Sit at my right hand, until I make your enemies your footstool for your feet.

Daniel 7:13-14 (WEB): "I saw in the night visions, and behold, there came with the clouds of the sky one like a son of man, and he came even to the Ancient of Days, and they brought him near before him. [14] Dominion was given him, and glory, and a kingdom, that all the peoples, nations, and languages should serve him. His dominion is an everlasting dominion, which will not pass away, and his kingdom one that will not be destroyed.

Another central claim for the religion is that the Trinity is not biblical, while the Scriptures demonstrates otherwise. Without the Trinity God the Father is a self-existing, distant, and unapproachable nomad. There is no love for the world, that also prompted the Father to send Jesus to save us, therefore there is no salvation by grace through faith, no forgiveness of sins through Jesus' shed blood, and no Holy Spirit to draw us to Him. There can be no relationship between God and humanity. In essence, we are doomed and there is no hope of redemption and eternal life with God, which explains the demeanor of the *average* Jehovah's Witness, but not all are *average*. Some are still searching.

Matthew 3:13-17 (WEB): Then Jesus came from Galilee to the Jordan to John, to be baptized by him. [14] But John would have hindered him, saying, "I need to be baptized by you, and you come to me?" [15] But Jesus, answering, said to him, "Allow it now, for this is the fitting way for us to fulfill all righteousness." Then he allowed him. [16] Jesus, when he was baptized, went up directly from the water: and behold, the heavens were opened to him. He saw the Spirit of God descending as a dove, and coming on him. [17] Behold, a voice out of the heavens said, "This is my beloved Son, with whom I am well pleased." (Also, Mark 1:9-11, Luke 3:21-22)

I was recently watching a full movie on a Saturday morning, when my doorbell rang. I ignored it expecting my husband to answer. He was still upstairs, so he didn't. Slightly annoyed, I went towards the door and saw that there were Jehovah's Witnesses standing on my porch. I quickly opened the glass door and politely said to them that I was a Christian and that I had no interest in a religion that denied the deity of Jesus Christ. With surprised or concerned looks on their faces, both ladies nodded as a sign of their understanding of my position and prepared to leave. I didn't wait to see them turn to leave because I had already closed the door and rushed back to my movie. After my movie ended, I felt some conviction regarding not having dialogue with them, so I casually but sincerely asked Abba to give me another chance.

Later that morning, my husband and I went to walk the trail at a nearby park. My husband was done before me, so he went to wait for me in the car. As I came to the end of my walk, I saw two female Jehovah's Witnesses set up right off the trail for ministry at the park. I have never seen that before. I am pretty sure that a county park has rules against such, but there they were. Of course, my first inclination was to walk right past them, but I was reminded of my promise to take advantage of the opportunity if presented with it again, so I approached the ladies.

I wasn't in a hurry this time. I was willing to engage in conversation. I had no prepared speech, and I really didn't know what I would say. I merely made myself available for, I didn't know what, at the time. I approached the ladies and mentioned the contention between Christianity and their religion's denial of Christ being God. The younger woman took the lead. She may have been a new or recent convert. She was a beautiful and pleasant soul, inside and in appearance. There was a brightness about her, unlike anything that I had ever witnessed among Saturday morning Witnesses.

She asked me to give her Bible verses, from my Bible where Jesus claimed to be God and I could not recall anything. My mind went blank. She pulled out her phone and pulled up the Bible and basically started tapping her feet, waiting for me to give her a verse, any verse, her Bible, my Bible, any Bible that substantiated my belief, but I could not. My mind was blank.

I sincerely can't recall the exact exchange in this moment, but it landed on something to do with commitment to reading or studying the Scriptures regularly, but the Holy Spirit chimed in. I made a confession. I disclosed to the young woman that I had been committed to reading the Bible almost daily for over thirty years, but that a few days earlier while on this same walking trail, the Holy Spirit had revealed to me that with all of my early morning Bible readings, I was still "mean", therefore there is more to it than reading and studying the Bible. I obviously had not consistently allowed the Holy Spirit into these times of reading.

John 16:13 (WEB): However, when he, the Spirit of truth, has come, he will guide you into all truth, for he will not speak from himself; but whatever he hears, he will speak. He will declare to you things that are coming.

The young woman was stunned by my words. Her eyes watered as she stared into mine. My confession disarmed her. I don't understand what Holy Spirit did, but He did something. She softened and we had a meaningful exchange. To my surprise, afterwards, the young woman asked me for my phone number. I had a feeling that it was against the rules, but she didn't care. I was her new best friend at that moment. It was obvious that she had her own mind.

On the other hand, like the high priest, many other Jehovah's Witnesses are blinded to spiritual truth because they aren't looking for truth. They are seeking to preserve a lie and trained to proof text specifically for the purpose of trying to prove that Jesus is not God. This seems to be the purpose for the founding of the religion, consequently thereby making it diabolical. The Bible is a spiritual book, and it is foolishness to those who are not looking for the truth, so Truth is hidden from them.

1 Corinthians 1:18 (WEB): For the word of the cross is foolishness to those who are dying, but to us who are being saved it is the power of God.

The hospice patient and her adult daughter were both lovely people, very pleasant. However, I knew from past experiences that the goal for them was to share their faith with me. Therefore, I showed up every two weeks, and we discussed life and religion. The patient was primarily a quiet observer, while her daughter did the subtle witnessing.

1 John 4:1-3 (WEB): Beloved, don't believe every spirit, but test the spirits, whether they are of God, because many false prophets have gone out into the world. [2] By this you know the Spirit of God: every spirit who confesses that Jesus Christ has come in the flesh is of God, [3] and every spirit who doesn't confess that Jesus Christ has come in the flesh is not of God; and this is the spirit of the Antichrist, of whom you have heard that it comes. Now it is in the world already.

The founder of the religion was under the influence of the spirit of the antichrist. Many of the followers of the religion are also under the same spirit, according to above Scripture, along with every other religion or person that does not affirm both the full deity and the full humanity of Jesus Christ. Jesus was not just a prophet, great teacher, or advocate for the poor. He is God incarnate, the Savior of the world. Dare to seek the truth, whatever your beliefs are. Eternity is a long time.

POW! (Pearls of Wisdom): True Christianity might cost you your families, friends, and more.

Chapter 14
Service Connection

I got off the elevator on the floor that housed the veterans with mental health issues at a VA Medical Center. I used my card key to open the door and headed back to the most secure area of the unit. The veterans in this area were considered the most mentally compromised. I was there to conduct a spiritual assessment on a veteran who was admitted overnight.

After checking in with the nursing staff, I proceeded to the veteran's room. There was a young woman standing near the door outside his room. She was a small framed young woman with piercing blue eyes. Her eyes stood out to me because of the intensity of her stare. I wasn't sure if her demeanor was due to her mental health situation or the medication that she was likely taking for the situation.

Before I entered the veteran's room, the woman asked if I would come to her room and pray for her. In retrospect, I don't know how she knew that I was the chaplain. I wasn't dressed in clergy attire, and she didn't seem capable of assessing such information. I assured her that I would come with her after my visit with the other veteran.

I completed my visit with the first veteran and exited his room. The young woman was still outside his room. Her private room was across the hall. I led the way into her room, and she followed. This was rookie mistake number two. I was in the room of a mentally challenged patient with no clear path to the door. Rookie mistake number one was that I did not check in with the nursing staff regarding my intent to visit her in her room.

The young woman and I stood in her room facing towards each other. I stood close to the head of her bed while she stood near the door. It was my practice to ask for specific prayer requests, but I don't remember what she requested. As I prayed for her, she continued to gaze at me with her head slowly tilting from side to side as if she was studying me. Her behavior was strange, so I never closed my eyes either. I watched her as she watched me as I prayed. After I finished praying, she asked me for a Bible. I ended my visit and dropped off the Bible later that day.

I had another spiritual assessment in this unit a few days later, so I checked in with the nursing staff, and I was surprised by what she shared with me. She shared that the young woman with the piercing blue eyes whom I visited a few days prior had a history of violence. She had attacked other staff who entered her room, including her psychiatrist and a nurse.

She shared that she had watched my encounter with the young woman on the surveillance camera which was set up in the young woman's room. The more compromised veterans had cameras in their rooms. The nurse shared that she was surprised that the young woman had not attacked me as she had the others who entered her room.

She reported that the woman had not been violent with anyone since my initial visit. She had slept with the Bible under her pillow since she received it, and I was shocked by what I heard. The nurse had patiently watched me on surveillance camera with the woman and waited to see the show. She waited for the young woman to attack me and never considered coming to the room to warn me. I didn't have any business in the young woman's room without first checking in with the nursing staff, but she could have come to warn me just in case.

I have considered since that time that perhaps the young woman or the spirit guiding her, had invited me into her room, also for the purpose of attacking me in private. I don't know. In retrospect, I was so excited that Jesus was willing to use me that I didn't have the sense to take proper precautions at times.

I was in the unit again a few days later, and the young woman approached me again for prayer. She asked me if my husband and I could return to her room and pray for her again. Of course, I did, but I continued to ponder what she said. No one else had been with me the first time I entered her room to pray. And then it dawned on me. Jesus had been in her room with me that day, or He sent an angel to stand with me.

Hebrews 1:14 (WEB): Aren't they all serving spirits, sent out to do service for the sake of those who will inherit salvation?

The patient saw in the spirit what was hidden from me in the natural. It explains why she had stared and studied me so intently like I had two heads. She saw two heads, mine and some otherworldly Being that was also present. It also explains why she did not attack me. I had help in the room, and she saw Him.

Psalm 91:11 (WEB): For he will put his angels in charge of you, to guard you in all your ways.

Mental illness had to stand down in the presence of Divinity. Also, the God of the Bible captured and arrested her, and she wanted Him to stay, which is why she asked for the Bible and slept with it under her pillow. The Bible was a symbol of Jesus' presence to her and the deliverance that Jesus granted her on that day. That Bible became a comfort to her. The nurse reported that she slept with it under her pillow from that day forward and that she didn't have any more violent outbursts.

I do not know if the young woman maintained her deliverance and stayed in her right mind or not after she was discharged, but if so, she would have had to make some tough decisions. Sustained deliverance would have meant forfeiting her VA benefits if they were connected to her compromised mental health. A rarely discussed reality regarding being a faithful Christ follower is that it costs us something. In this case, the young woman's VA benefits were at stake if she experienced complete healing from the mental illness.

Matthew 16:24 (WEB): Then Jesus said to his disciples, "If anyone desires to come after me, let him deny himself, take up his cross, and follow me.

A person in this situation would then need to reject deliverance and pretend NOT to be mentally well to keep the checks and the other benefits coming. The act of lying about such is ok and even encouraged among the veteran population, but that is not God's way. There have been veterans who started the journey to securing their service-connected benefits by way of deception because it's easier to disprove physical disabilities than mental issues. Unfortunately, they played with mental illness enough that it became real. Deception gives an invitation to a whole new set of spiritual issues. Jesus warns that discipleship is not without cost.

POW! (Pearls of Wisdom): Salvation is free but walking it out will cost you.

Chapter 15

Identity Crisis

I drove up the steep driveway that led to the hospice patient's home. The terminally ill patient was a husband and father of middle school-aged children. His wife was his primary caregiver. As a hospice chaplain, I was there to continue chaplain visits that were started by the previous chaplain. I don't believe the family specifically wanted the visits, but the conditions of their hospice care benefits likely made them feel obligated to accept the service.

My visits with this family were straightforward. My one-on-one visits with the patient could take less than five minutes. The patient's wife spoke English, but I was told that the patient did not. The patient could no longer communicate using words anyway. The terminal illness had taken its toll.

The patient's wife was very pleasant. She would greet me at the door and escort me to the patient's bedside when I arrived for visits. Depending on her schedule, she would either leave me alone with the patient or stay with us. I would pray or say blessings over the patient and let myself out if she was busy.

This was my first chaplain job after my chaplain residency, where I was exposed to various kinds of spiritual care interventions. I was still eager to try out various ways of connecting with families according to their religiosity, apparently even to my own spiritual harm at times. I remember the look of horror on a hospice team member's face, who was also Christian, when I told her that I was familiar with Reiki and willing to learn and practice it on patients who had a desire for it.

The new patient and his family practiced Hinduism, so I wanted to connect with them accordingly. I pulled out a book from my previous World Religions class, brushed up on the basics, and proceeded to provide spiritual support to this family accordingly. I also went online and printed some prayers that were found in some of the religion's sacred texts. I was always looking for new prayers or blessings to pray over him. I went deeper and deeper into the different types of prayers until Jesus intervened.

On my last visit with the patient, I sat in the car going over the prayers that I was planning to speak over him, and I was interrupted and warned against moving forward with the prayer. As I rehearsed the prayer, Jesus simply said, "You better not." and I felt the urgency of the warning. It was the same feeling I had when I was warned about another situation. At that time, I considered tasting the red veggie concoction made specifically for me by a fellow chaplain, who was also a witch. She was previously in a chaplain cohort with me.

She identified as a wiccan witch. She initially pushed the "good witch" narrative, but her pride got the best of her. She disclosed that she also had the means and power to work spiritual wickedness and cause harm to others when necessary. She was a good witch, but with enough spiritual dark clout to release wrath on those who came against her, with the aid of her four deities, she claimed.

To demonstrate her spiritual wickedness and prowess, she invited leaders from her coven to come to our cohort to do didactics on some of the tools of the trade including root working, works with crystals, and other schemes of wickedness. Under the guise of spiritual inclusivity, the cohorts' grades, including mine, were contingent upon our individual receptivity to the wickedness of this woman's spiritual manipulations.

Fortunately, I was somewhat familiar with her tactics. When I was a child, some of my relatives were entangled in some of these practices, in one way or another. Therefore, I had a general idea of the dangers of her practices, so I never played into them.

She was at one extreme of spirituality, and I was at the other, but she worked fervently to close that gap.

Leviticus 19:31 (WEB): "'Don't turn to those who are mediums, nor to the wizards. Don't seek them out, to be defiled by them. I am Yahweh your God.

She randomly gave me a pair of earrings, but Abba warned me to get rid of them. When I threw them in the trash at my house, Holy Spirit instructed me to get them out of my house. Throwing them in my Herby Curby was not sufficient. I had to drive to the mall parking lot and throw them in the trash there. There were likely demons attached to them.

Revelation 21:8 (WEB): But for the cowardly, unbelieving, sinners, abominable, murderers, sexually immoral, sorcerers, idolaters, and all liars, their part is in the lake that burns with fire and sulfur, which is the second death.

She also brought me a bowl of a red veggie concoction that she prepared especially for me. I was a vegetarian at the time and so was she. Surely, she noticed that I never tasted the other tasty treats that she provided for potluck, so she made something special for me. I took the red concoction home with me, understanding that I was going to throw it out, but my naivety got the best of me.

I decided that I would taste a drop of it, so that I wouldn't be lying when I reported to her how it tasted. It was when I preceded to open the container that the ceiling of my small house seemingly rolled back, and Father spoke to me out of heaven warning me not to taste the stew. He said to me, "You better not!" The next day at work, Father confirmed to me that the witch had put blood from her menstrual cycle in the stew.

She was very crafty. There was never any open conflict between us. She worked her magic incognito, but Jesus protected me. She once told me that she *knew* that I was a *real* Christian. I suspected that she ran into a roadblock when her astral projection travels failed to gain her entry into my home when she tried to visit illegally.

Isaiah 59:19b (KJV): When the enemy shall come in like a flood, the Spirit of the Lord shall lift up a standard against him.

I don't believe she was deceived in terms of believing that these entities that she was involved with were good. She was deep in her craft. She had certainly encountered angelic forces that battle on behalf of the heirs of salvation, so she was clear about the difference, but she liked the allusions of control that these practices awarded her.

People, including Christians, mix their faith with black magic, white magic, witchcraft, sage, crystals, incense, fortune telling, tarot cards, mediums, psychics, and other dark arts because they want to control people and situations. For many, Christianity is not an option for these reasons. Jesus is Lord, and we are subject to His plan and the timing of His plan for us. Not even prayer and fasting can force Jesus to submit to our plans, while these spirit guides can make evil plans come true, at a wicked witch's command, to an extent.

The entities she seemingly employed could wreak havoc, even on Christians who are unwise to their tactics as I partly was. My story would have likely ended differently if I had eaten her red concoction, worn her jewelry, or willingly and actively participated in her other schemes. In retrospect my prayer life likely aided and saved me. Holy Spirit led me to intercede for my team members daily, wiccan witch included. I didn't have a clear idea of what I was dealing with, but Jesus did.

The witch was literally trying to kill me. I have no medical issues, but I had two severe fake medical diagnoses during my time working with her, one involved my heart and the other my bladder. I got a second opinion on the bladder situation, and it was deemed a ridiculous misdiagnosis. The heart monitor that I had to wear for a week also didn't confirm any issues with my heart.

I only connected the dots to her regarding the health scare later. One of the other chaplains communicated to me that the witch bragged about her practice of retaliatory magic that targeted the hearts and or organs of those who opposed her.

Isaiah 54:17 (WEB): No weapon that is formed against you will prevail; and you will condemn every tongue that rises against you in judgement, This the heritage of Yahweh's servants, and their righteousness is of me, says Yahweh.

The way she bewitched the leadership of the chaplain department was not fake at all. I am still traumatized by the way the leadership turned on me because of her bewitching. They were eating out of her hand, allowing her to defile anything sacred that she set her sights on.

They allowed her to do whatever she wanted in the name of religious inclusion. If we could have a Good Friday service, she could have a New Moon ceremony. Abba kept me safe in spite of all of this. He demonstrated to me in different ways that she would not prevail in her attacks against me. The name of the town where I lived during this time was called Mount Carmel, TN, the name of the mountain where God gave Elijah victory over the prophets of Baal and Asherah; the false prophets who ate at Jezebel's table (1 Kings 18).

The wicked wiccan witch's reign finally came to an end when the new chaplain chief arrived. He was a strong conservative Christian Believer with a twenty plus year military leadership career and a no-nonsense spiritual approach to service; the right one for this situation. He strategically shut her and every wicked thing she brought with her down to the ground.

So, understandably, I never read the Hindu prayers over the patient after the warning. The Holy Spirit responds to prayer, but apparently, so do Hindu demons disguised as deities, which is why I was warned not to continue with the prayers. They were prevented from harming me, but the game could have changed if I had unknowingly continued conjuring them up or communicating directly with them via my prayers. Understandably, I abandoned the practice of trying to connect on this level.

However, during my visit with this Hindu patient on this day, I decided that I wanted to sneak in a Jesus prayer instead, since the Hindu prayer was out. I did not want to violate his freedom of choice of religion, but I couldn't help myself. He didn't understand English, so I couldn't ask him anyway. I wanted to see what would happen.

As soon as I began to pray to Jesus, Jesus made His presence known. I did not see Him, but His brilliance apparently pierced the spiritual darkness of the room. The patient was bedbound, but he would have jumped to his feet if he could have.

He never tried to speak to me during my visits because he couldn't. The terminal illness had taken his ability to verbally communicate. We didn't speak the same language anyway. He would follow me with his eyes as I approached him with a welcoming demeanor, but something different happened during this visit. When I began to pray, he jumped to attention and stared at me with an accusatory stare on his face. Something had gone awry in his spiritual world, and he understood that my prayer was the culprit. Busted, I stopped praying and quietly observed his continued response for a few minutes.

He was visibly offended. Jesus had burst onto the scene to show him that there is "Someone" greater than all the demons disguised as deities whose presence he had grown accustomed to, but he didn't want to know. He didn't like the interruption. I ended my visit shortly afterwards, and I don't remember ever visiting him again. I transferred to a different office, so he was no longer my patient. I remember hearing when he passed over.

Ezekiel 18:32 (WEB): For I have no pleasure in the death of him who dies," says the Lord Yahweh. "Therefore turn yourselves, and live!

This patient was steeped in Hinduism, but it was likely not his fault. He had no control over where he was born, who he was born to, or the religious culture that raised him. He was likely born into Hinduism, and Abba understands such things, which is why He sends others. I know that I was not the first or only one sent to this patient throughout his lifetime.

Matthew 12:46-50 (WEB): While he was yet speaking to the multitudes, behold, his mother and his brothers stood outside, seeking to speak to him. [47] One said to him, "Behold, your mother and your brothers stand outside, seeking to speak to you."[48] But he answered him who spoke to him, "Who is my mother? Who are my brothers?" [49] He stretched out his hand toward his disciples, and said, "Behold, my mother and my brothers! [50] For whoever does the will of my Father who is in heaven, he is my brother, and sister, and mother."

This patient had a type of dementia, so he was limited in his communication, but he was fully capable of deciding his spirituality. Jesus assured me of such later in my chaplain career. This patient was not born with a frayed brain. It was a side effect of his illness. His rational mind could not express itself in words to me or others, but he had full access to the Lord spiritually, as the Lord had full access to Him.

Jesus revealed Himself to him on this day for sure, but he didn't want to know Truth, at the time. It would have cost him something; his spiritual identity, which he seemingly did not want to part with at that time.

POW! (Pearls of Wisdom): Have nothing to do with the dark arts and false religions nor join in with those who practice them. You are inviting demons into your home; your bodily home and where your children sleep.

Chapter 16

Questionable Companionship

I rang the doorbell, and a middle-aged woman came to the door and invited me inside. It was New Year's Eve, but there were no signs of newness in the home. The father had been diagnosed with a terminal illness, and in his case, with only a few more days to live. I was there to assess the spiritual needs of the patient and his family.

The new hospice patient's wife completed the assessment with me. The patient was in the bedroom resting and I wasn't invited to meet him. Religion or spirituality was not a present reality for him nor the rest of the family at this time. There had been a break in their spiritual fellowship.

The patient's wife shared that, as a couple, she and the patient had begun their journey together as active Christians attending a church that the patient's father pastored. His grandfather had pastored the church before his father. Once they were married, the patient also pastored the church. They began raising their boys in that same church.

She disclosed with some difficulty that a few years into the marriage, the patient decided that he no longer believed in the God of the Bible. He resigned from his position as pastor of the church, and they all stopped attending church altogether. The patient never disclosed his reason for turning away from Jesus, and his wife said that she never asked. She blindly followed.

Disconnected from their faith community, they found community within the activities that their upper-middle-class lifestyle afforded them, things that they didn't have time for when they were tied to the church. The patient's son was drafted onto a major league baseball team. The family began traveling to see him play. It was their new religion.

The patient's wife was overwhelmed by regret as she verbalized her husband's turn from the God of the Bible. This was seemingly also the first time she realized that she had done the same. She had also turned away from Jesus. She turned when he turned. He led, and like a good Christian pastor's wife, she followed and probably thought she was doing the right thing at the time. I don't think she had ever saw it in that light; her conformity being equivalent to her turning from Jesus as well. Each person is responsible for his/her individual decisions. Ananias and Sapphira are perfect examples of that. Couples are not judged by God as a team, but as individuals.

Acts 5:1-10 (Amplified): But a certain man named Ananias, with Sapphira his wife, sold a possession, [2] and kept back part of the price, his wife also being aware of it, then brought a certain part and laid it at the apostles' feet. [3] But Peter said, "Ananias, why has Satan filled your heart to lie to the Holy Spirit and to keep back part of the price of the land? [4] While you kept it, didn't it remain your own? After it was sold, wasn't it in your power? How is it that you have conceived this thing in your heart? You haven't lied to men, but to God." [5] Ananias, hearing these words, fell down and died. Great fear came on all who heard these things. [6] The young men arose and wrapped him up, and they carried him out and buried him. [7] About three hours later, his wife, not knowing what had happened, came in. [8] Peter answered her, "Tell me whether you sold the land for so much." She said, "Yes, for so much." [9] But Peter asked her, "How is it that you have agreed together to tempt the Spirit of the Lord? Behold, the feet of those who have buried your husband are at the door, and they will carry you out." [10] She fell down immediately at his feet and died. The young men came in and found her dead, and they carried her out and buried her by her husband.

The patient's wife was visibly saddened by the fact that she had also unknowingly turned away from God, and their children also followed. She was only realizing at this moment that she could have gone to church and continued without her husband. She could have continued her relationship with the Lord, because it seemed that at this point, she didn't have one either.

Her husband also had not forbidden her from pursuing relationship with Jesus. It was no longer his personal desire, but she was free to pursue her personal spiritual desires. Her biggest regret was that she never explored with her husband why he turned, and now it was too late. He passed away later that evening.

In the months that followed, she shared that she was tormented because she feared that her husband went to Hell, *into the fire that shall never be quenched, where their worm does not die, and the fire is not quenched (Mark 9:43, 44)*. The human heart is resilient and can bounce back from death and loss, especially under normal circumstances, but her grief was complicated by extenuating circumstances. She had not explored conversations with her husband regarding his turn from Jesus. I provided spiritual care to another pastor's wife who had a similar experience.

I also provided grief care to her following the death of her husband. As my visits with her continued, I realized that she had not approached her relationship with her husband as if he was a man that she was married to but as if she was a devoted God appointed servant to him in his role as pastor. She revered and respected him as her pastor too much to see him as a mere mortal.

He was an image of the invisible God to her. She also had some ambivalence regarding his spirituality that she never questioned while he was alive. She also didn't know what he believed, specifically, and she also never dared to ask. She was honored to have been in service to him as his wife, but her glory left when he died. It was only after the death of their husbands that these wives realized what kind of marriages they had surrendered themselves and their service to. The two women seemingly thought that their husbands were mediators for them between themselves and God. I considered that both ladies may have had the same issue. They both made idols of their husbands.

Exodus 20:3 (WEB): "You shall have no other gods before me.

After the deaths of their husbands, both were faced with the reality that they didn't know Jesus, which made the grieving process more difficult. Jesus didn't have a chance with either of them until after their husbands were gone. This is a cautionary tale for other wives who operate as they did.

POW! (Pearls of Wisdom): Each person is responsible for their own relationship with Jesus. Your spouse can't present you before the Father without spot or wrinkle; only Jesus can.

Section Five
Golden Girls

Chapter 17

Scorned Woman

I entered the assisted living facility to see a hospice patient. She wasn't a new hospice patient, but this was my first time visiting her. The previous chaplain had possibly had chaplain visits with her. She had early-onset dementia and had lived in the assisted living facility for several years. She was nonverbal and dependent on others for her complete care. She had no children. Her ex-husband was her only family.

To customize my spiritual care plan for her, I called her ex-husband to inquire about her spirituality, or lack thereof, her favorite music genre or artists, and other random things about her. He reported that she was Presbyterian and a huge Elton John fan.

She was previously a churchgoer, so I also began reading a Christian devotional to her, *Jesus Calling*. The devotional book has 365 devotions, one for every day of the year. I read this devotional to most of my Christian dementia patients. It was through these readings that I realized that Holy Spirit was still speaking, specifically to these patients. I was surprised at what He had to say during some of my insightful moments with them.

I initially had so much pity for this patient that I never considered anything but how sorry I felt for her. We all felt it. It was common knowledge that her husband had divorced her for the purpose of qualifying her for residency in this upper scale assisted living facility, which is not uncommon. The problem was that he then married her best friend, but that was still not the worst part of it. They both came together almost daily to have lunch with the patient. Her ex-husband considered the patient a "turnip," so he didn't think it mattered.

This patient grew accustomed to our pity. She had dementia, but her wits were intact. She used her illness to her advantage. She couldn't speak with her mouth, per se, but she had ways of communicating what she couldn't say with words, at times. I learned that if she didn't want to be bothered by someone, she wouldn't respond to them, or she did respond, but with a blank stare. She initially did this to me. She pretended to be a "turnip".

I tried the music that her husband suggested, but she showed no interest. At the time, I didn't realize that she had the ability to show interest. On this visit, an unexpected song came up on my playlist, and I allowed it to play. It was a song that would have been entirely unfamiliar to her in her normal context.

The song was equivalent to an old negro spiritual. It was gritty, and it was long. It lasted over nine minutes and the last four were of the artist howling, but I couldn't bring myself to turn it off. I let it play and when it was finally done, I offered an apology to the patient, and she burst out laughing.

I was shocked. It was then that I realized that she could communicate if she chose to do so. Since I had her attention, I changed up the playlist and played some contemporary gospel music, including CeeCee Winans, and her response continued to be strong, with periodic sounds of approval here and there.

I was so shocked that I approached the staff with this news. I asked the nurses who took care of her if they knew that she had the ability to engage with others as I discovered and that she liked contemporary gospel music. Of course, they knew. They were with her daily. They were also the ones who inadvertently introduced the music to her. It was the music that they listened to while taking care of her. Their music became her music.

The nine minute song that I felt compelled to let play for her was entitled "*I Won't Complain.*" I discovered that the irresistible force that compelled me to allow this extended version of this song to play in its entirety was, indeed, the Holy Spirit. He was addressing the patient's attitude about her situation. The patient had apparently gotten into some serious self-pitying, but Jesus didn't see her situation the same way she and most of us did.

Psalm 139:13-14 (WEB): For you formed my inmost being. You knit me together in my mother's womb. [14] I will give thanks to you, for I am fearfully and wonderfully made. Your works are wonderful. My soul knows that very well.

The Holy Spirit had me communicate to her that while she had seemingly been dealt a bad hand; dementia, divorce, abandonment, and eating from the hand that stole her husband, she still had to choose Jesus if she didn't want to leave this earthly life of pain and suffering only to enter into the next place that would be worse if she didn't reset her heart, forgive, and make Jesus her choice. I didn't have a conversation with her about Hell, but I verbalized to her what I believed the Lord wanted me to say, and I believe she received it. It was not a "Let's be best friends." moment, but I am confident that she understood what was being communicated to her. Her response told me that it may have been hard for her to hear, but she received it. She was a smart lady.

Philippians 1:6 (WEB): being confident of this very thing, that he who began a good work in you will complete it until the day of Jesus Christ.

It makes sense that she and other dementia patients are still intellectually and spiritually present. I just never thought about it. I was too busy pitying her. She was still a sinner in need of the Savior, and not even her heartbreaking circumstances were enough to secure her salvation without acknowledgement that Jesus is her Lord and Savior. She also had to forgive like all other sinners looking to Jesus for mercy and forgiveness. Her debilitating illness was not a free pass to salvation.

Of course, this is not true of those born intellectually disabled; without the capacity to know right from wrong and intellectually stuck in a child-like mindset. They are pure in heart, and they shall see God (Matthew 5:8). For others, God's grace is sufficient to cover all disappointments, heartbreaks, sins, and betrayals, but only when we put our trust in Jesus as Savior, dementia or no dementia.

My encounter with her revolutionized my hospice chaplaincy ministry. I had initially resisted hospice chaplaincy as a career. It was a slower pace than I wanted. If the hospice company had more patients on the census, I likely would not have had visits with as many dementia and nonverbal patients, but that was Jesus at work. The dementia patients added meaning to my hospice chaplaincy career. When I recognized that Abba was working, I began seeking out these types of patients. I secretly considered myself "the dementia patient whisperer".

Most families were diligent in meeting the physical needs of their loved ones with dementia, but not so much emotionally, mentally, and spiritually. The dementia patients were pieces of furniture to some of the families. Many families, like this patient's ex-husband, just didn't believe that there was someone still inside.

When this patient died, I called her ex-husband, to extend my condolences. He expressed to me that she was better off because she was just a "turnip" and had no quality of life anyway. *"Quality of life according to who?"*, I shouted, but he didn't hear my thoughts.

I went on to share my experiences with her, her laughter, her love of gospel music, and how she used her illness to dismiss those whom she didn't want to be bothered with. He was shocked and speechless for several seconds. I suspect that his mind went back to all the times that she had stared at him and her best friend with a blank stare.

The Holy Spirit taught me that if a dementia patient has unassisted breath in their body, they are still alive and in their right mind. Hence, they are still responsible for choosing Jesus and where they want to spend eternity. It is not automatic. If a dementia patient is still breathing, Jesus is still working their case.

Abba also taught me that illness is not always about the patient but that He is always at work redeeming someone or something. In essence, Father God will even use a terminally ill hospice patient to bring redemption to others. We don't always have a choice in how God wants to use us.

Philippians 2:10-11 (WEB): that at the name of Jesus every knee should bow, of those in heaven, those on earth, and those under the earth, [11] and that every tongue should confess that Jesus Christ is Lord, to the glory of God the Father.

His love for humanity is such that He uses every possible circumstance to facilitate redemption and to draw us to Himself. He sets up the opportunities, but the decision belongs to the individual. I am confident that this patient made the right choice. She was able to lay down her self-pity and to reconcile with Jesus.

POW! (Pearls of Wisdom): If a person is still breathing without artificial mechanisms, they are still alive. Holy Spirit is still working, therefore, so should you.

Chapter 18

Grief Growl

I arrived at the home of a returning hospice patient to conduct a spiritual assessment. She was previously dropped from service because she no longer fit the criteria for hospice care. Her terminal illness certainly had not progressed in the way originally anticipated, which is death within six months.

She was in her seventh year of hospice care when she was dropped. Her longevity surely had much to do with the exceptional care that her family ensured she received, in addition to the mercy of God. Hospice patients who are valued and loved by their families and caregivers seem to live longer than those who are not. Dying of a broken heart is a real thing. The pain of abandonment is painful to sit with in such a state.

I once provided spiritual care to a faithful Catholic woman whose consistent prayer request was that God hurry her transition, thereby, transporting her to her heavenly home as soon as possible. She had a private room in an exceptional personal care home, but it wasn't her home, so she never emotionally adjusted to her new reality.

She had relocated from a different state with hope and expectation of living out her last days with her son and his family. When her health began to fail, her son moved her into the personal care home, and it broke her heart. Unfortunately, she was not a dementia patient, so she was acutely aware of everything that was happening in her life.

She was still well enough to leave the personal care home. She was available for lunch or outings with family and to spend the weekend with them, but she was left hanging. They didn't seem to want to be bothered with her, and she never grew accustomed to the abandonment.

She had spent her resources, emotional and material, on great schools and lifestyle upgrades for her three children, but they had no time for her in her time of need, which greatly impacted her will to live. In my experience of taking spiritual care of hospice patients, they rarely spoke ill of the children who had essentially abandoned them. The truth about the situation was probably too painful to hear from their own lips. On the other hand, I didn't judge the families in these cases.

Ma Ma and Pa Pa were sweet and lovely elderly women and men of God when I encountered them. I don't know what they were like as younger parents, but I don't think it matters to God. He commands us to honor them, regardless, and the commandment comes with a promise. God understands that honoring dishonorable parents is a true sacrifice. Therefore, we are not commanded to honor them because they all deserve honor. It is one of those "do it because I said so" situations, and we will be blessed by God for the sacrifice.

Ephesians 6:2-3 (WEB): "Honor your father and mother," which is the first commandment with a promise: [3] "that it may be well with you, and you may live long on the earth."

The returning patient's husband greeted me at the door, as he had many times before. His bride of over sixty years was suffering from dementia. They had been churchgoing people and had served their faith community well. He shared that they had enjoyed a good life. They met in college, traveled the world, had great careers, a successful business, a faithful church community, and three devoted daughters. Life had given them exceptional returns, but I don't believe the patient felt the same.

1 Peter 5:6-7 (WEB): Humble yourselves therefore under the mighty hand of God, that he may exalt you in due time, [7] casting all your worries on him, because he cares for you.

The patient was bedbound, nonverbal, and dependent on others for her complete care. There was a paid caregiver in the home, to say "bless you" if she sneezed or to wipe away tears that periodically gathered in the corners of her eyes. She was provided with phenomenal care. I started fresh and ascertained from her husband her likes and preferences in terms of how she previously cultivated her spirituality and other details that would help me to design a spiritual care plan for her.

My interventions with her included music by Elvis Presley and Patsy Kline. I also read poetry to her and the Bible. Things were going well. She was nonverbal and unable to effectively communicate with others, but her husband shared with me that the patient liked me and that she enjoyed my visits. I discerned the same, but I noticed that while she enjoyed the music and poetry, she didn't seem to like it as much when I read the Bible or other religious texts to her.

I was also reading the *Jesus Calling* 365-day devotional to her, and that's when her demeanor would change. I noticed some angst within her. She didn't appreciate these readings. Abba used these devotional readings to give me insight about the patients, but more importantly, insight on how to address the spiritual issues afflicting them.

Listen. Jesus is committed to coming into the darkest of places to "see about" us. We can't go dark or deep enough that Jesus will not take off His robe and sandals to come and get down in the thing with us to talk us up and out of the emotional, mental, and spiritual pits that we dig ourselves down into. This insight is also how I know that dementia patients are still intellectually present. I don't know what the science or research on dementia patients show, but Jesus informed me that they are cognizant and not only capable but still required to decide where they want to spend eternity.

Matthew 16:17 (WEB): Jesus answered him, "Blessed are you, Simon Bar Jonah, for flesh and blood has not revealed this to you, but my Father who is in heaven.

This patient was understandably disappointed regarding her life being snatched by dementia and likely a few other things. Abba instructed me to address it with her. I addressed her disappointment, and everything changed after that. She no longer tolerated my visits. She spent the remaining time that I was with her grimacing and growling with her teeth clenched. It was very unnerving for me.

I grew up watching the original *Exorcist*, starring Linda Blair and other movies like that, so I wasn't comfortable with attempting to cast anything out of her. I was not prepared to deal with a spinning head and green vomit being spewed in my face.

I was not bold enough to cast it out of her, but I whispered the name of Jesus during my time with her. I may have even whispered, commanding the demon to come out of her, but nothing happened. The growling continued. I whispered because her husband kept a baby monitor at her bedside. He was very protective of her. I didn't want to cause a ruckus, so I whispered Jesus' name for my own protection. The patient had seemingly already chosen her side. She refused to be comforted.

In retrospect, her husband knew about these demonic manifestations, which is why he didn't go near her. He walked past the living room several times a day but would not go in and spend time with her. I noticed this earlier in my visits, when my time with the patient was still going well.

At that time, I had suggested to her husband that he begin spending time with the patient and he resisted my suggestion. With conviction, he disclosed that he prayed for her faithfully every night when his head hit his pillow. The demonic manifestations are probably what he prayed about because he wouldn't go near her. The paid caregivers were her constant companions, but they went home during the night hours. The patient slept in a hospital bed downstairs alone in the living room while her husband slept upstairs with his head under the covers, hoping not to further stir up those growling spirits.

Philippians 4:8 (WEB): Finally, brothers, whatever things are true, whatever things are honorable, whatever things are just, whatever things are pure, whatever things are lovely, whatever things are of good report: if there is any virtue and if there is anything worthy of praise, think about these things.

The patient also likely growled at him or did worse, but for different reasons, which is likely how he knew that she liked me. She didn't growl at me initially. He knew her well enough to know her different temperaments, but he would not have spoken to me about such. His image of a good life couldn't include demonic manifestations.

He knew more about her potential pain than I could have. He wasn't the type to share those kinds of details about their life or marital challenges. He took pride in the comfortable life that he had worked for. He only shared the good times, vacations in Europe, golfing in the Carolinas, and skiing in Aspen.

The last time I visited this family, the patient was still growling and meditating on her disappointments. Her husband stopped taking my calls and receiving my chaplain visits. We never discussed it, but he likely heard the growls during my visits. He recognized that something changed regarding the patient's response to me. Understandably, he didn't want her peace interrupted so he discreetly ended my visits with her, and I never questioned it. I was no longer with the company when she passed away.

POW! (Pearls of Wisdom): Jesus understands our disappointments. Talk to Him. You don't need words.

Chapter 19
Sound of Despair

The new hospice patient lived a little further out than most of the others, so it took a little longer for me to arrive at her home. She was actively transitioning, so it was important for staff to get there as soon as possible. She wasn't going to live much longer.

The patient's husband provided me with the information I needed for my spiritual assessment. The patient was a Christian, and her brother-in-law was a pastor, so hospice sponsored spiritual care was declined. Before ending my visit, the patient's husband escorted back to the bedroom to see the patient. She was already primarily unresponsive but breathing disturbingly loud.

The paid caregiver was still sitting with her, and a black cat was also keeping watch over the patient. The curtains were closed, so her room was dark. It also felt dark. It was a creepy scene. The cat startled me when he suddenly leaped up on the bed with the patient and walked around her in protection mode.

Matthew 11:28 (WEB): "Come to me, all you who labor and are heavily burdened, and I will give you rest.

The patient's husband disclosed that the patient had given up on life a year prior after their adult daughter committed suicide. Their daughter had moved back home after being discharged from the military. The suicide took place in their home. The patient's husband disclosed that his wife never recovered from the death of their only child. After speaking with the patient's husband for a short while, I ended my visit.

Proverbs 4:23 (WEB): Keep your heart with all diligence, for out of it is the wellspring of life.

Early the following morning, I received a call from the patient's husband. He asked me if I could come over right away.

He had declined hospice-sponsored spiritual support but said he desired another visit from me. He needed help with something.

Overnight, he had heard some disturbing sounds coming from the patient's room that alarmed him. He was a button-down shirt, khaki pants-wearing insurance guy. He didn't use any dark language to describe the situation, but it sounded like he suspected demonic activity in the patient's room.

I still had no direct experience with this sort of thing, but I am a born-again Christian Believer in Jesus Christ, so I took my anointing oil and drove over. The patient was still unresponsive, but some hair-raising sounds were coming out of her, horrid growling. It was unnerving, but at least her husband and I agreed that something demonic was present, although there was no verbal acknowledgement. I knew the name of Jesus was my weapon, so I prayed for her, telling the evil spirit to leave, in Jesus Name and it did.

It wasn't anything dramatic. Her bedroom did not become a scene from *The Exorcist* like I previously feared. I didn't raise my voice or do anything extra and nor did the evil spirit that was oppressing her. Jesus obviously entered the scene because the demonic presence left without a fight. The sounds stopped. There was no visible evidence that anything happened, only her husband's emphatic gratitude that he continued to show me for months following the patient's death.

Families are offered an additional year of grief support or spiritual wellness calls and visits after the death of hospice patients. Most of the families just didn't answer their phones when I called, in favor of just moving on with their lives without my call to remind them of the pain of loss. This wasn't the case with this patient's husband.

He picked up his phone every time I called him, and he fully engaged in conversation with me. He was relieved that his wife was finally at peace. He even sent the company a letter expressing his appreciation for my spiritual care. Of course, he never mentioned anything about the patient's *situation*. He was a button-down shirt and khaki pants-wearing insurance guy.

His wife was a Christian, but she sunk so low into depression that it took over her person, leading me to revisit the Bible verse that addresses a spirit of heaviness. Meditating on the disappointment of her daughter's suicide month after month after month gave place to the devil. The devil does not miss an opportunity to oppress anyone, even a Christian. He moved in on her until the name of Jesus forced him to leave.

Isaiah 61:1-3 (KJV): The Spirit of the Lord God is upon me; because the Lord hath anointed me to preach good tidings unto the meek; he hath sent me to bind up the brokenhearted, to proclaim liberty to the captives, and the opening of the prison to them that are bound; ² To proclaim the acceptable year of the Lord, and the day of vengeance of our God; to comfort all that mourn; ³ To appoint unto them that mourn in Zion, to give unto them beauty for ashes, the oil of joy for mourning, the garment of praise for the spirit of heaviness; that they might be called trees of righteousness, the planting of the Lord, that he might be glorified.

The evil spirit was trespassing and had no legal extended rights to her. He was not invited to Heaven with her, so he had to go before takeoff. He saw weakness and moved in on the patient while she was in despair. The patient was a Christian Believer before her daughter's suicide. She had an opportunity to reset once Jesus ran off the evil spirit. She passed away later that evening. The Father's love kept her alive until she could get to her spiritual self.

POW! (Pearls of Wisdom): Your depression might also be a "spirit" of heaviness. Tell it to go from you, in the name of Jesus and see if your medication works better.

Chapter 20
Faulty Faith

The street in front of the new hospice patient's home was filled with cars when I arrived for the spiritual assessment. When I approached the front door, it swung open, and a family member enthusiastically invited me inside. The house was filled with family and friends from the patient's faith community. The patient and her husband were pastors of a local congregation.

The patient's terminal illness was not new, but the terminal label had been rejected. The family had faith and expected that she would fully recover and resume her life as it was before the illness. Therefore, hospice care was called in at the last hour. The patient was already transitioning, but her family and friends were unwilling to let her go. They refused to give up hope for her full recovery.

They had gathered at her home to pray for a miracle. I could hear and feel the energy of fervent prayer as I entered the home. I was escorted to the bedside of the new patient, where I stood with the others who were gathered around her bed. Space was made for me, close enough for me to hold her hand. She slipped her hand into mine as I approached.

The patient's husband, who was leading the prayer, paused long enough to introduce me, and then continued in prayer. I continued spiritually assessing the patient, her family, and the situation. The patient was a Christian Believer, and so were the others who gathered to pray on her behalf. The patient's eyes locked into mine, and they told me a different story from what I heard in the prayers. She understood that she was going to a better place, sooner rather than later, but that she had to leave this world to get there, and she was ok with that.

The patient and I had an immediate connection, so we sat in that space together while her husband waged war against the terminal illness and anything that came against his faith or his ideas of what her healing should look like. I understood that the patient was in a different space. She accepted that her life on earth had come to an end, and she wanted someone to help the others to understand the same. She looked to me to do it, but we both understood that her husband couldn't receive such.

2 Corinthians 5:1-8 (WEB): For we know that if the earthly house of our tent is dissolved, we have a building from God, a house not made with hands, eternal, in the heavens. ² For most certainly in this we groan, longing to be clothed with our habitation which is from heaven, ³ if indeed being clothed, we will not be found naked. ⁴ For indeed we who are in this tent do groan, being burdened, not that we desire to be unclothed, but that we desire to be clothed, that what is mortal may be swallowed up by life. ⁵ Now he who made us for this very thing is God, who also gave to us the down payment of the Spirit. ⁶ Therefore we are always confident and know that while we are at home in the body, we are absent from the Lord; ⁷ for we walk by faith, not by sight. ⁸ We are courageous, I say, and are willing rather to be absent from the body and to be at home with the Lord.

I had no words for the situation. My heart was heavy, so the only intervention I had to offer was presence. As my visit came to an end, the patient's husband asked me if I would say a closing prayer. I agreed and began to pray, ultimately asking that God's will be done in hopes of prepping him for the inevitable, but he rejected my prayer. Her husband went ballistic at the sound of my words. He interrupted my prayer and scolded me for not praying in faith.

Stunned, I suggested to him that he pray and that I would agree with his prayer instead. It was only Holy Spirit who directed my words in this way because I was like a deer in the headlights. His passionate interruption frightened me, but Abba rebounded the moment. The patient's husband ended his prayer, and shortly afterwards, I ended my visit.

The patient transitioned the following day. She couldn't wait any longer for her husband and the others to agree. She adjusted her faith and placed it in its rightful place, the God of her faith. We need faith to successfully engage in a relationship with Jesus, but in situations like this, many Christian Believers allow faith to overshadow God. Faith becomes an idol, exalted above God. Without faith, it is impossible to please God, but faith is not God.

Hebrews 11:6 (WEB): Without faith it is impossible to be well pleasing to him, for he who comes to God must believe that he exists, and that he is a rewarder of those who seek him.

The reward is that Jesus will respond to belief and fervent pursuit of Him, but there is no guarantee that we will like the response. Nevertheless, there will be a response; yes, no, maybe, wait, etc. Yes, a Believer can speak to a mountain, and it will be removed and cast into the sea, but not if the finger of God is holding it in place because it is not His will that it move.

Mark 11:23 (WEB): For most certainly I tell you, whoever may tell this mountain, 'Be taken up and cast into the sea,' and doesn't doubt in his heart, but believes that what he says is happening, he shall have whatever he says.

Therefore, whenever a Christian Believer has a situation, it is wise to allow the Holy Spirit to reveal His will in the situation. It is important to ask Jesus what He wants to do about it and then agree by praying according to His revealed will about the situation. This is how we get our prayers answered, by agreeing with God. It is also permissible to ask God to change His mind, but there is no guarantee that He will.

God communicated to David via Nathan, the prophet (2 Samuel 12), that he was going to allow his son to die. David prayed in hopes that God would relent, but God did not. The boy died, and the boy had done nothing wrong, which is often the case with many others. We do nothing wrong to deserve some of these things. Adversity is a consequence of living in a broken world as broken people. Our time on earth merely expires. God communicated to Hezekiah (2 Kings 20) via Isaiah, the prophet, that he was going to die. Hezekiah prayed, and God lengthened his days.

Job 14:5 (WEB): Seeing his days are determined, the number of his months is with you, and you have appointed his bounds that he can't pass.

The Bible is filled with prayers detailing the promises of God and instances when God moved in miraculous ways on behalf of all sorts of people. We are free to grab whichever random promises we want, but it is wise to check with God to see if a particular promise is *His* will for *us* in *our specific* situation.

Many are the afflictions of the righteous, but the Lord delivers him out of them all (Psalm 34:19), but you must ask Abba what deliverance looks like for "you." Yes, pray that you and your family *prosper in all things and be in health* (3 John 1:2), but ask Abba what prospering in all things and being in health looks like for "you." *Healing is indeed the children's bread* (Matt 15:26), but again, you must ask Abba what healing looks like for "you."

A few years ago, I discovered a lump in my breast. Since I was in the process of changing employers, I didn't go to the doctor right away. I waited for my insurance to start with the new company. For the almost two months that I waited, my subconscious mind settled on me dying. I wasn't sad about it. It was just something that I was willing to accept as fact. I shared with my husband that if diagnosed with breast cancer, I would not fight the illness or death. I informed him that I would submit to the dying process without a fight.

I have this theory that until it is an individual's God-ordained time to die, all the angelic forces of heaven work overtime to hold back death, waking up the person who has fallen asleep while driving, leading another one to take a day off work on the day of the explosion, or redirecting the route home on the day that the bridge collapsed. People die, not necessarily because they've done something wrong. God is not punishing us when someone we love dies. Their time on the earth or in this dimension is just over.

Supernatural beings are at war around us, angelic beings fighting for us and evil beings and the hosts of wickedness fighting against us, although the natural eye cannot always see them.

Ephesians 6:10-12 (WEB): Finally,[1]be strong in the Lord, and in the strength of his might. [11] Put on the whole armor of God, that ye may be able to stand against the wiles of the devil. [12] For our wrestling is not against flesh and blood, but against the principalities, against the powers, against the world-rulers of this darkness, against the spiritual hosts of wickedness in the heavenly places.

We all have stories of times when we would have been harmed, injured, and even killed if not for a mysterious intervention of some sort. We escaped death because it was not our time to die. On the other hand, I believe that when it is time, the protective forces stand down and death comes and is successful. When it's time, there is no escaping the car accident, drowning, accidental overdose, or slipping away while asleep, for the most part.

I had come to believe that my time was ending, so I accepted it with no questions asked, but it was not my time. Just for the record, I do not believe that suicides and abortions are God-ordained death strategies. Of course, they don't catch God by surprise, but I don't believe that they are ever His will.

Ecclesiastes 7:17 (WEB): Don't be too wicked, neither be foolish. Why should you die before your time?

I eventually went to my primary care doctor's appointment, and she scheduled me for a mammogram and a sonogram immediately. The appointments were scheduled for the same day and in the same building. I was familiar with the mammographer because I had a standing yearly appointment with her. In the past, we chatted it up, but this time was different. She had a look of concern on her face as she conducted the exam. There was no conversation, just retake after retake. After the exam, she gave me a "pink" folder to take with me downstairs to the sonographer.

When I arrived downstairs, they were waiting for me. I wasn't required to sit and wait. The nurse immediately escorted me back to an exam room where two others were waiting. They also had long faces. They gave me one or two directives and then nothing. Again, this was concerning. There was no chatting in effort to make me feel at ease. Again, there was retake after retake after retake. Afterwards, I was instructed to go back downstairs to the reception area, where I waited. And now the receptionist had a long face. I stayed there for a while and then was told that I would hear from my primary care doctor.

By this time, I was pretty sure that I would be diagnosed with cancer. I was convinced that my life was ending, so I didn't think about or pray about it specifically. I wasn't concerned about it, so I was surprised when Abba broached the subject with me. I was on my knees praying about some other random things when Holy Spirit interjected a thought into my mind; *"You are planning to die, and you never asked Me if it is My will."*

Surprised, my spirit revived. I wasn't aware that I was submitting to death prematurely. It had never occurred to me to ask Abba His will in the situation, so I was filled with hope because of His interruption. Faith filled my heart, so I aligned my heart with the will of God. I began to resist the spirit of death that I had embraced in my heart and with my words.

At this time, Jesus did not reveal to me that I didn't have cancer, only that it wasn't His will for me to die because of this situation. I also understood that if He wanted me to fight through cancer treatments, then that was what I would have been required to do, but I wasn't going to die from it. In that moment, I understood that Jesus is in control of how healing would take place for me. In essence, He was reminding me of my initial commitment to submission to His Lordship over my life.

1 Corinthians 6:19-20 (WEB): Or don't you know that your body is a temple of the Holy Spirit who is in you, whom you have from God? You are not your own, [20] for you were bought with a price. Therefore glorify God in your body and in your spirit, which are God's.

Thankfully, cancer was not a battle that I had to fight. God's word made the difference between life and death for me. He interrupted my surrender to death and breathed the will to live into me, and then I developed a fighting faith, but I had God's Word as my reinforcement. I then added faith to this situation because the Holy Spirit told me what He wanted to do. He shared with me what His will was in the situation, so I agreed with Him. I just needed to walk in that specific word spoken to me about this specific thing. At this point, I became anxious to hear my results. I wasn't sad or angry; just ready to face it and to fight, if necessary.

I called my doctor's office for my results the next day or so. The nurse placed me on a long hold. When she returned to the phone, she said that my lab results were coming through fax at the exact time of my call. I don't believe that was a coincidence. The initial results were held back until I aligned with the will of the Lord, thereby being adjusted to reflect God's will. The nurse reported that everything looked good. There was nothing for me to be concerned about. No breast cancer! Of course, I was grateful, and I praised Jesus for the deliverance.

The experience gave me life-changing insight into 1 John 5:14-15, thereby changing how I approach prayer. If we pray according to God's will, we have what we ask for every time. Unfortunately, I can't say that I initially prayed God's will in this situation because I didn't know God's will and never thought to ask. Thankfully, Holy Spirit interrupted my submission to a premature death and revealed His will to me, and I prayed accordingly. When I aligned with God's will, there was no cancer diagnosis. Discovering God's will in this situation was the game-changer, not my faith in faith. The moral of the story is that we are to ask Jesus for His will in every situation and then pray accordingly.

I must add that I subconsciously accepted breast cancer and premature death because of a mistake that I made earlier in my life. I believe it was before I was a Christian, but I'm not sure. I was in my early twenties. A friend encouraged me to get a numerology reading, so I did. My friend gathered my numbers and submitted them to the woman. I didn't know better. I don't remember anything else about the numerologist's report except the time of my predicted death. It was thirty years into the future, so I seemingly forgot about it, but not really.

I subconsciously, kept the age of my supposed death tucked away in the back of my mind. I discovered the lump in my breast about two years before that age. I figured that without a fight, the cancer would take about two years to take its toll and then I would be gone. When the lump appeared, I considered that I had forever cursed myself when I consulted with the numerologist, but Jesus overturned the verdict because He is merciful. It wasn't my God-ordained time to die.

I sincerely believe that I would have received a breast cancer diagnosis and would have died if Jesus had not interrupted the pack that I had made with the devil to die a premature death. Discovering and praying God's expressed will in specific situations makes the difference.

POW! (Pearls of Wisdom): A recipe for success in getting your prayers answered is to agree with Jesus' specific and revealed will to "you" about "your specific" situation.

Chapter 21

Overcomer

I drove through the entrance of the gated community where the new patient lived. The neighborhood was quiet and uneventful, very peaceful. The landscaping was perfectly manicured like a picture in a magazine. I parked my car in front of the garage doors and walked onto the front porch, where the housekeeper was waiting. They were expecting me. The housekeeper invited me inside and offered me something to drink while escorting me to the sunroom.

I was at the home of a new hospice patient for the purpose of conducting a spiritual assessment. Unbeknownst to me, I was coming to the end of my hospice chaplain career, as I knew it. I entered the hospice care industry reluctantly. My dream chaplain job was back in the hospital or VA medical center settings.

There was more hope in these settings; hope of recovery and living even if not always so happily ever after, nevertheless still living. Hospice care offered the hope of a "good death"; a death that was free from physical pain despite terminal illness, nevertheless still death. It was a hard reality for most families, especially Christians. By Abba's design, hospice care was simply the first place that would hire me after my chaplain residency.

It was during my visit with this patient that I began to understand why I had been sent to hospice care. Like the other hospice patients, I was sent there to die, hopefully a "good death". Also, like many of the hospice patients, my transition took longer than six months and more than one hospice care company to get me there.

John 12:24-26 (WEB): Most certainly I tell you, unless a grain of wheat falls into the earth and dies, it remains by itself alone. But if it dies, it bears much fruit. ^{25} He who loves his life will lose it. He who hates his life in this world will keep it to eternal life. ^{26} If anyone serves me, let him follow me. Where I am, there my servant will also be. If anyone serves me, the Father will honor him.

This patient had been diagnosed with cancer, but she declined the treatment options. She had a choice of allowing either Chemo or cancer to have its way with her body. She opted for cancer this time. She did not want another bout with Chemo, she disclosed.

She identified as a Christian Believer and was at peace with dying. She felt that she had lived a good life and had no complaints to register. She lived alone but had a paid housekeeper who came by to take care of random things. The patient was also legally blind and not allowed to drive.

She had two sons who lived in neighboring states with responsibilities that prevented them from visiting often. They relied on others to supplement their absences. They eventually placed the patient in an assisted living facility.

The patient was in relatively good health, aside from the cancer. She had a peaceful presence about her that suggested that she had discovered the secret to life but had no compulsion to broadcast it. She was a pampered Southern belle without a care in the world, not even cancer. I was drawn to her because of her unusual resolve and confident calmness.

I settled into my visit with the patient and initiated storytelling. She was in hospice care because of cancer, but she had also suffered multiple other health crises throughout her lifetime and a slew of other trials and tribulations. I was in awe as I heard the details.

The most incredible thing about the patient was that she was untethered by the tragic things that had happened in her life. The scar on her left cheek was merely a conversation piece for her at this point. She had been brutally raped and beaten and her husband murdered during a home invasion years prior, but there was no evidence of residual trauma from that. She was not emotionally distraught as she told her story. She was not bitter. She was not angry with Abba.

She was a pleasant, faith-filled woman whose faith in Jesus was completely intact. She had rolled with life's sucker punches, kicks, and death blows, but she was no longer moved by them. She was the opposite of me, and this was the primary reason why I was sent to hospice care. I needed an up-close look at what overcoming adversity, repeatedly and without residue, looked like. There were likely other patients who displayed this same resolve, but this was the only time that it registered.

I have had my share of adversity, but not in comparison to what the patient shared with me. Fortunately, Abba knows His children. I would have probably jumped off a bridge into rush hour traffic if I had experienced what this patient described to me.

Once, when I was not offered the job that I interviewed three times for, I asked my husband to hide my handgun because rage suggested to me that I shoot myself. I still hear the gut grunt that came out of my husband's soul when I told him my thoughts. I then had to contend with fantasies of strangling myself with a rope; the kind of rope used to hang delinquents in Western movies.

The thought of a coarse rope tearing through the skin and flesh on my throat gave me satisfaction. Sounds crazy, right? What sound-minded person would entertain hurting themselves, their loved ones, and Abba in this way. Who wants to feel or inflict that kind of pain?

Mark 12:30-31 (WEB): You shall love the Lord your God with all your heart, with all your soul, with all your mind, and with all your strength.' This is the first commandment. [31] The second is like this: 'You shall love your neighbor as yourself.' There is no other commandment greater than these."

Obviously, the thought of gratification associated with me violently attacking my own body originated from elsewhere. The deceptive thought came from outside my rational mind. The thought was fleeting, but alarming to me. The source of this kind of foolishness came from the devil himself; the father of lies.

John 8:44 (WEB): You are of your father the devil, and you want to do the desires of your father. He was a murderer from the beginning, and doesn't stand in the truth, because there is no truth in him. When he speaks a lie, he speaks on his own; for he is a liar, and the father of lies.

There had been times throughout my life that I wished I could just fade out of existence, but suicide had never been a real consideration for me. Interestingly, I don't recall having such thoughts before I was a Christian. This fact deserves more exploration, but not now.

Since I am a Christian Believer, Jesus is my Lord and Savior, therefore as Lord, He determines when my life on the earth is over. I am unwilling to face the possible consequences awaiting me if I violate that agreement by taking my own life into my own hands on this level. The essence of Christianity is the complete surrendering to Jesus' Lordship. Therefore, it is not my life to take or to end.

1 Corinthians 6:19-20 (WEB): Or don't you know that your body is a temple of the Holy Spirit who is in you, whom you have from God? You are not your own, [20] for you were bought with a price. Therefore glorify God in your body and in your spirit, which are God's.

I personally don't want to believe that suicide is a direct trip to Hell, but that Abba deals with it on a case-by-case basis. On the other hand, what I know for sure is that Abba would never tell or suggest to anyone that suicide is His will for any individual, regardless of how heinous their transgressions have been. Therefore, anyone considering such is being influenced by the devil and that has never led anyone to a good place. Remember, he is the father of lies.

Luke 10:19 (WEB): Behold, I give you authority to tread on serpents and scorpions, and over all the power of the enemy. Nothing will in any way hurt you.

It is not worth it to commit suicide to escape pain in this life, and then to possibly be fast tracked to a place that is inconceivably worse and that you can't wake up out of. Trouble doesn't last always. Morning is coming. It is not as bad as it seems. If you pause and give it some thought, you'll see that the father of lies is also exploiting your pain.

Psalm 30:5b (KJV): weeping may endure for a night, but joy cometh in the morning.

Destructive thoughts originated within me because of disappointment. I was disappointed when I didn't get what I had prayed, cried, fasted, and asked Abba for. It was devastatingly personal to me when certain doors were closed off from me, primarily doors regarding my career aspirations. I felt abandoned by Abba when certain things didn't happen for me and the devil never fails to try and exploit such. His goal was and remains to turn humankind away from Jesus and everything the devil does in this world is designed to lead humankind to that dead end, ultimately to reject Jesus; causing us to believe that God does not care about what happens to us.

I don't enjoy and nor do I want to talk about this evil one. I would prefer to live my life without ever thinking about him. He would like that even better, but I realized that he was way more active in my life than I understood. He wasn't flipping over cars, burning down my house, or killing off my family members. His attacks are much more subtle than that, which is why I didn't understand that I was under attack and have been, essentially, all my life. We are all targets of his subtle wickedness.

Again, the thought for me to shoot myself was alarming, which is why I shared it with my husband. I didn't recognize it as the devil. It was even more alarming to my husband because he likely considered that I was probably more capable of shooting someone else than I was of shooting myself. Such thoughts were out of character for me, but the devil is not afraid to fail. He shot his shot with me to see if it would land and he tries to deceive everyone in some way or another.

Consider a time when you had a ridiculously depraved or alarming thought…that was him. We don't have complete control of what pops into our thoughts, but Christian Believers have more control of our responses. Those who have not surrendered to the Lordship of Jesus Christ are puppets with the father of lies as their puppet master, so it's a little different.

The devil has access, but it is limited in terms of what he can do to Christian Believers because we don't belong to him. If he gains ground in the Christian Believer's life, it is usually because unrepentant sin gave him access. We have been adopted into Abba's family. Christian Believers are God's property, flawed, yet still God's business. Fortunately, all humanity has access to this same relationship, but it's a choice.

Galatians 4:4-7 (WEB): But when the fullness of the time came, God sent out his Son, born to a woman, born under the law, ⁵ that he might redeem those who were under the law, that we might receive the adoption as children. ⁶ And because you are children, God sent out the Spirit of his Son into your hearts, crying, "Abba, Father!" [7] So you are no longer a bondservant, but a son; and if a son, then an heir of God through Christ.

Therefore, the devil's primary strategy with Christian Believers is to talk us into doing ourselves harm, emotionally, financially, physically, and many other ways, beginning with a thought. He talks us into sabotaging ourselves. Trickery is a sport to him. Again, he is not afraid to fail. He tried to tempt Jesus, God incarnate.

Matthew 4:1-11 (WEB): Then Jesus was led up by the Spirit into the wilderness to be tempted by the devil. [2] When he had fasted forty days and forty nights, he was hungry afterward. [3] The tempter came and said to him, "If you are the Son of God, command that these stones become bread." [4] But he answered, "It is written, 'Man shall not live by bread alone, but by every word that proceeds out of God's mouth.'" [5] Then the devil took him into the holy city. He set him on the pinnacle of the temple, [6] and said to him, "If you are the Son of God, throw yourself down, for it is written, 'He will command his angels concerning you,' and, 'On their hands they will bear you up, so that you don't dash your foot against a stone.'" [7] Jesus said to him, "Again, it is written, 'You shall not test the Lord, your God.'" [8] Again, the devil took him to an exceedingly high mountain, and showed him all the kingdoms of the world and their glory. [9] He said to him, "I will give you all of these things, if you will fall down and worship me." [10] Then Jesus said to him, "Get behind me, Satan! For it is written, 'You shall worship the Lord your God, and you shall serve him only.'" [11] Then the devil left him, and behold, angels came and served him.

By the time I encountered this patient, I was on a repeat cycle of disappointment-despair, like many of the patients whom I was serving, at the time. Since life is filled with big and small disappointments, I could never get a handle on my feelings of despair. I was stuck. The devil was relentless in giving me his commentary against Jesus regarding every disappointment and everything else and I unknowingly leaned into his deception.

This cycle had been among the reasons why I had not been willing to fight back against the possible breast cancer diagnosis years earlier. I was gripped by despair due to the lies of the father of lies. I did not understand the role the devil was playing in my feelings of despair, consequently, I felt abandoned by Abba each time my hopes and dreams were delayed, denied, or dashed. He is a master at playing mind games. Jesus had to also contend with feelings of abandonment. He shouted it out from the cross.

Mark 15:32-34 (WEB): Let the Christ, the King of Israel, now come down from the cross, that we may see and believe him." Those who were crucified with him also insulted him. ³³ When the sixth hour had come, there was darkness over the whole land until the ninth hour. ³⁴ At the ninth hour Jesus cried with a loud voice, saying, "Eloi, Eloi, lama sabachthani?" which is, being interpreted, "My God, my God, why have you forsaken me?"

Jesus felt what we feel while on the cross, but He didn't retreat. The sinless Savior went on to secure salvation for the world, but his humanity felt what was happening to Him, physically and psychologically on the cross.

Years ago, I preached a sermonette on one of the last words of Jesus for an Easter/Resurrection Day service and I made mention that Jesus battled psychologically on the cross and senior chaplain colleagues stopped talking to me, specifically the licensed psychiatrist, who was also in the chaplain cohort. She later disclosed to me that she had a problem with me saying that Jesus battle psychologically on the cross, but I didn't say it. The Scripture does.

Hebrews 4:15 (WEB): For we don't have a high priest who can't be touched with the feeling of our infirmities, but one who has been in all points tempted like we are, yet without sin.

This patient had also not allowed disappointment to derail her from God's expected end for her. There was no evidence of her past or present disappointments. She was living well, despite past and present circumstances. She had conquered the voice of the enemy in her affairs and now she was being used by Abba to help bring awareness and deliverance to me so that I too could also begin living in victory.

1 Corinthians 10:13 (WEB): No temptation has taken you except what is common to man. God is faithful, who will not allow you to be tempted above what you are able, but will with the temptation also make the way of escape, that you may be able to endure it.

As I marveled at her strength and resolve, I felt Abba's presence. He whispered into my spirit, *"If you live in this world, there will be adversity...BUT as my child, you overcome."* And like the water waves that backwash from a rocky coastline, the Holy Spirit washed over me, taking with Him, the spirit of despair and heaviness that had lodged themselves into my soul.

Abba gave me understanding that life does not come without challenge. Therefore, disappointments are inevitable during the human experience, but as a Christian Believer, I was a destined Overcomer. In essence, I was being called to mature in this area. This moment marked the beginning of the end of my bondage to disappointment-despair.

1 Corinthians 13:11 (WEB): When I was a child, I spoke as a child, I felt as a child, I thought as a child. Now that I have become a man, I have put away childish things.

Over time, I became progressively more aware of how and when my thoughts are being invaded by rogue thoughts. These thoughts are lies against Abba and contrary to His character. A line of defense against the devil's attacks is to submit our lives to Jesus, thereby making resistance possible. We don't have a chance of overcoming out there on our own.

The Bible tells us to resist the devil, and he will abandon his attack. However, we must understand that resistance is not a one-time deal and nor is submitting to Jesus' Lordship. Submitting to Jesus is a lifestyle. We must also continuously resist the devil, because he will certainly return with something else at some point.

James 4:7 (ASV): Be subject therefore unto God; but resist the devil, and he will flee from you.

More importantly, we must understand that the father of lies is actively seeking to take us down and eventually out of the eternal presence and purpose of God. This is how he had such success and impact in my life, and in the life of many others.

Hosea 4:6a (WEB): My people are destroyed for lack of knowledge...

There was no awareness, on my part, regarding the mental and emotional devilish manipulation I suffered, while the Scripture is clear regarding our need to watch for him. We don't need to overwhelm ourselves by looking for him out there in the world somewhere, but he infiltrates on a much more personal level than that. The devil attacks our thought-life, often using our own voice or the voice of a trusted friend or family member to do so.

I have never been one to espouse "the devil is trying to kill me" narrative. I have never seen myself as someone the devil considers a threat, but I am and so is every other person who bears witness to the name of Jesus. Unfortunately, I lived my life oblivious to the reality of the role he played in influencing my thoughts and emotions. The Scripture calls for us to be more vigilant than that. None of us have the luxury of ignoring his desire to devour us.

1 Peter 5:8 (WEB): Be sober and self-controlled. Be watchful. Your adversary, the devil, walks around like a roaring lion, seeking whom he may devour.

His goal is to keep individuals away from relationship with Jesus, by any means granted to him because misery loves company. I think it is less about us and more about his hostility towards Jesus. Afterall, what have we as human beings literally ever done to him? It still hurts my heart to remember such, but I have a context for how the devil's hostility towards the children of God and other human beings possibly works.

I was born to a mother who wasn't quite emotionally prepared for me. I came about at a bad time for her, and she never got over the inconvenience of my conception and birth into her failing marriage. She didn't have the same feelings for me as she had for my siblings and I felt it from the beginning, even from the womb. They have research that speaks to the impact of a mother's emotionality on her unborn child.

Since my mother loved them and not me, I manifested jealousy and anger towards them, causing me to strike out violently against them, at times. Of course, I didn't understand back then, but I hurt them because my mother loved them. I couldn't make her pay personally for emotionally disowning me. My strength and power were no match for my mother's, so I hurt her by striking out against them. I hurt what she loved.

I believe that this is how the devil operates and why he seeks to destroy human beings in this way. He wants to hurt human beings because God loves us. There is no possibility of redemption for him. He is permanently separated from God. He is unredeemable, while overcomers will one day reign with Jesus.

Revelation 3:21 (WEB): He who overcomes, I will give to him to sit down with me on my throne, as I also overcame and sat down with my Father on his throne.

Among other reasons, I was sentenced to hospice chaplaincy for the purpose of the terminal cycle of disappointment-despair being exposed for what it was, spiritually motivated. My encounter with this patient brought me awareness that I was being manipulated by the enemy's lies. Fortunately, I was delivered, consequently, instigating the shift in my capacity to trust Abba again in ways that I didn't realize I had stopped.

John 3:16 (WEB): For God so loved the world, that he gave his only born Son, that whoever believes in him should not perish, but have eternal life.

My chaplain encounters were also used by Abba to restore what I lost in seminary; my conviction, that Jesus is the *only* way to God for all of humanity. It is my conviction that no other religious path leads to the living God. I would be remiss if I didn't clearly say, especially at a time when there is so much deception. We owe it to ourselves to search the matter completely, regardless of religious tradition. In the meantime, Jesus loves you and there's nothing you can do about it!

POW! (Pearls of Wisdom): You are an Overcomer, but ultimately, only in Christ Jesus!

Author's Info

ReShaping Faith Publishing, LLC
4002 Highway 78, Suite 530-213
Snellville, Georgia 30039
reshapingfaith.com
reshapingfaith@yahoo.com

Thanks for your review on Amazon!

www.ingramcontent.com/pod-product-compliance
Lightning Source LLC
Chambersburg PA
CBHW051626120626
46551CB00014B/1949